Reconstructing Architecture for the Twenty-First Century

An Inquiry into the Architect's World

This volume is an eloquent and farsighted call for a new approach to thinking about, producing, and inhabiting architecture. Using a richly conceived architectural history as a means for analysing debates that reverberate throughout the arts and human sciences, Anthony Jackson examines the myths of the architectural profession and in so doing reveals how they have arisen out of particular relations of power in a world shifting from autocracy to democracy.

Jackson exposes the inadequacies of old conceptions of architecture as embodying metaphysical properties, and of architects as being the sole keepers of this esoteric knowledge. He challenges architects to acknowledge and celebrate building as an expression of the ideals and values of the broader-based classless communities to which they now belong. The less people are excluded from the design process, the more likely it is to be effective in bringing about a human-made environment that enriches the lives of its inhabitants.

In examining intersecting ideas about myth, culture, class, and design, the author draws examples from a wide array of architectural styles, ranging from Classical to Post-Modern. The result is a work that is extraordinarily provocative and useful for architects, visual artists, cultural historians, and sociologists, as well as for supporters of all forms of participatory democracy.

ANTHONY JACKSON is a professor in the Faculty of Architecture at the Technical University of Nova Scotia.

ANTHONY JACKSON

Reconstructing Architecture for the Twenty-First Century

An Inquiry into the Architect's World

UNIVERSITY OF TORONTO PRESS

Toronto Buffalo London

© University of Toronto Press Incorporated 1995
Toronto Buffalo London

Canadian Cataloguing in Publication Data

Jackson, Anthony, 1926–
    Reconstructing architecture for the twenty-first century :
    an inquiry into the architect's world

    Includes bibliographical references and index.
    ISBN 0-8020-0625-6 (bound) ISBN 0-8020-7584-3 (pbk.)

    1. Architecture. I. Title.

    NA2500.J33 1995   720   C95-930156-9

This book has been published with the help of a grant from the Canadian
Federation for the Humanities, using funds provided by the Social
Sciences and Humanities Research Council of Canada.

To the theorists in my family, Timothy and Naomi

Contents

Preface

It should be noted that the scope of the statements in this book is related to the way the subject is approached. Architects personally are as diverse as any other group, but the world of architecture, regarded as an institution, imposes basic characteristics on its participants. This allows generalizations to be made about the architectural profession as an entity. Similarly, where it is conceived as an art, architecture is usually assumed to have universal significance and relevance. It follows that generalizations are possible because art-world products are created and promoted in an international arena that largely ignores social or geographic boundaries. On the other hand, the organization and practice of architecture as a professional service varies considerably between countries. In this event, the locus of the argument is the English-speaking Western world.

The feminist movement has provided me with an instructive example by the passion and brilliance it has brought to its dissection of the past and its advocacy of new social ideals. A writer on architecture has a more difficult task. Women have entered enthusiastically into their debate because they have everything to gain. Architects are already part of the establishment and believe they have much to lose. They are accustomed to maintaining their position rather than questioning it. In this situation, Prince Charles is to be credited with encouraging a more open discussion of architectural issues.

I wish to thank Thomas Emodi and Andrew Saint for their comments on my manuscript, and Joan Bulger and Darlene Money for

their help in preparing it for publication. I am also grateful to the
Canada Council and the Canadian Federation for the Humanities for
their financial support.

Reconstructing Architecture for the
Twenty-First Century

1 The Problem

Architects should design buildings that support and enrich our everyday lives.

There is something very wrong with architecture as it is practised today. Architecture is not something rare that only the initiated can understand. It is just another name for buildings. Like other artefacts, buildings may be considered merely utilitarian or they may be enhanced by various means, such as decorating them to make them more visually attractive, or using them as images to evoke other sensations. In either case, they embody the values of the people who produce them.

Individuals generally accumulate possessions that suit their own temperaments. But most buildings (other than dwellings) are for communal activities. Collectively, they form towns for public use. In these circumstances, it is reasonable that buildings should reflect the values of at least the majority of the people who inhabit them. If they do not, there is a conflict between the public outlook and its constructed environment. Where buildings are in harmony with their society, they support and enrich its everyday life.

Unfortunately, the designs that architects produce primarily reflect their own preoccupations rather than the values of the communities they serve. This conflict of interests is so embedded in the historical development of the profession that even the word 'architecture' is a significant part of the problem. Like the term 'art,' architecture was long ago appropriated by a small group of self-appointed specialists and connoisseurs to categorize their own symbolic fare and separate it from other tastes. The converse of this strategy has been to belittle and exclude alternative types of experiences.

Architects exploit this artifice to differentiate their work from 'building.' Building, in their vocabulary, is mere construction, whereas architecture is building that embodies metaphysical significance. By denying all other buildings a proper name, they brand them as inferior or worthless. Only 'vernacular' architecture is admitted as an unsophisticated sort of folk-art. The bizarre consequence of this strategy is that the adjective 'popular' has been turned into a term of abuse. The connoisseur's measure of the worthlessness of the design of common artefacts – such as buildings and their furnishings – is for them to be liked by their everyday users.

This strategy has been so successful that standard definitions of art describe it as the application of skill to subjects based on taste or aesthetic principles. But words like art and architecture and 'good' taste and aesthetic principles are all interdependent and belong to the same conceptual package. Furthermore, these have been developed by a specific set of persons who make up the 'art world' and characterize themselves as artists or architects or connoisseurs or critics. In short, the producers and consumers of what is known as 'art' are the very people who have defined its terms of production and consumption.

The situation can be more readily understood if the term 'art' is redefined to describe any human product that evokes a meaningful response. It is then obvious that everyone responds to 'art,' not just a small élite. This can easily be seen by observing the impact of the market-place products that the art world finds most offensive. For example, radio songs have influenced the feelings of successive generations about love, romance, and sex. Movies like the Hollywood Westerns gave their audiences a lasting awareness of good and evil and redemption. Pottery figurines have brought pleasure and beauty to countless homes. These are no different in form and effect from the lieder, dramas, and sculpture that the art world promotes and markets for its own enlightenment. Their broad appeal shows the symbolic power of artefacts that lie outside the special set of products categorized as art by the art world.

These, in contrast, are considered so rare that they are seldom to be found, at least according to their leading advocates. Rather, charged with mystical qualities and treated like the museum pieces of the rest of the art world, architecture, it appears, exists solely for

the informed few. This arcane realm admits only exceptional buildings to its ranks. To be seen, they must be tracked across the world
or experienced vicariously through photographs and reviews. Architectural devotees are hard-pressed to find even a few buildings to
enthuse over in London or Paris or New York (cities that house
millions of inhabitants) and might travel through many populated
parts of the world without coming across anything worthy of their
interest.

This is absurd considering that architecture consists of the buildings that line the streets of our cities. It is also a biting commentary
on the capabilities of ordinary architects who, in this reading of
events, lack the skill to devise worthwhile designs. Most important,
it makes nonsense of the idea that architecture should support and
enrich the lives of the people who use it.

The reasons for this situation and its inherent incongruities are
embedded in the history of the profession, which shapes its current
practices. There are three different components to the architectural
scene. At the top is a small clique who belong to the art world and
determine the stylistic interests of the day. These are the designers
who, along with the critics, academics, and historians, are the current
creators of architectural doctrine. Below them is the rank and file of
the profession, with half an eye on their trend-setters, and the rest of
their energy concentrated on providing workable buildings for their
clients. Then, almost forgotten in the process, and largely outside it,
are the communities that occupy and, ultimately, are responsible for
the buildings that make up the towns in which we live.

The contention that architecture is rare is part of the politics of
exclusion that governs the activities of the art world. As an external
device, it keeps the uninitiated at bay. Used internally, it determines
the ranking system of the day. This factional infighting is not new,
nor are the verbal means by which it is carried out. Typically, it takes
place in two phases and at two scales.

First, the style to be supplanted is devalued. The pattern was set by
the Renaissance architect, Giorgio Vasari, who dismissed the earlier
Gothic style as 'monstrous and barbarous.'[1] This technique of dispar-
agement has proved to be effective in dislodging the prevailing style
to enable its replacement. In recent decades it has been used exten-

sively to discredit the Modern style, which has been accused of everything, from being trivial to brutalizing the lives of its occupants.[2]

An example of the way the method operates can be followed
through the autobiographical comments of the architectural historian
Vincent Scully.[3] Having designed his own house in 1950 in the Modern style, Scully subsequently became disillusioned with what he
viewed as the inferior work of the ordinary architects who used it.
His praise for the 'masters' of the Modern movement was seasoned
by erudite invective against their followers. The Modern style was
linked to the corporate world; its architects were portrayed as mind-
less bureaucrats; their buildings were denounced for being as syn-
thetic as the suits they wore. In 1964, Scully ridiculed the author
Norman Mailer for calling Modern architecture 'totalitarian.'[4] Two
years later, Scully was criticizing it in similar terms and endorsing
Robert Venturi for his advocacy of what became known as Post-
Modernism.[5]

Such conversions are usually explained as an intellectual advance,
where each new official style is advertised as an improvement on the
previous one (in what might be termed the technological analogy of
this year's model being better than the last). For instance, the critic
Peter Blake first wrote a eulogy on the achievements of the Modern
style and then recanted and condemned its failures.[6] In reality, what
changes is not the objective merit of the current style, measurable in
any technical or social benefits, but its underlying aesthetic values
and concerns.

Why and how these shifts in fashion take place is still virtually
unexplored, because their causes are unacknowledged in the mythology of art. It seems, however, that the capacity for change lies in the
composition of the perceptual elements that make up what we call
a style. Its images and ideas are intrinsically unstable and have their
own evolutionary potential. New links can be made, new combina-
tions formed. As the constituent parts of a style begin to lose their
mutual reinforcement, the style starts to lose its credibility. Not only
do our judgments change, but so does the very way we see. Buildings that once looked up-to-date and natural, come to look old-
fashioned and strange.

Even the aesthetic vocabulary alters. As was wryly pointed out in a magazine article at the end of the 1970s when the Modern style was giving way to Post-Modernism, architects no longer designed buildings but made 'interventions' in the urban environment; abstract art was out and 'semiotics' in; functional analysis had been superseded by a timeless 'typology' of forms that embodied the collective unconscious.[7] Under this regime, even a bad design in the new style is better than a good design in the old style that has been denounced by the experts.

If the initial step in establishing a new style is demolishing the old one, a concurrent goal is to eliminate possible competitors. Once again, the technique of verbal abuse is dominant, but in this case it is aimed at people rather than styles. Here, also, there are many precedents: Horace Walpole, who slandered Robert Adam, (one of the very few architects who had a style named after him); John Ruskin, who called A.W.N. Pugin 'one of the smallest possible or conceivable architects'; the proto-Modern architect Adolf Loos, who labelled the Art Nouveau architect, Henry van de Velde, 'pathological'; and in more recent years, the 'structuralist' Aldo van Eyck, who lashed out at everyone he despised in an attack on Rationalists, Post-Moderns, and other pests.[8]

An instructive example of eliminating competitors by denigrating their work was provided by the proponents of the Modern style. For the generation of architects that followed its dictates, any style that was not strictly Modern was suspect.[9] Hugo Häring was too organic, Willem Dudok was too traditional, Robert Mallet-Stevens was too frivolous, Buckminster Fuller was too radical, the architects of the American skyscrapers were too materialistic – not to mention the vast majority of architects who worked in various historical modes, who were simply dismissed as reactionaries.

Nor are those who design in an approved idiom safe from their zealous colleagues. Even here, the personal and occupational craving for recognition (and its rewards) that drives art-world advocates further limits their tolerance. So when Philip Johnson and Henry-Russell Hitchcock set down the rules of the Modern style to promote its virtues, Max Ernst Haefeli's stucco was found to be too rough, Karl Schneider's bricks too picturesque, and J.J.P. Oud's window frames too thick.[10]

The subsequent path of Oud's career further illustrates the intolerance in the world of art and architecture. One of the de Stijl group of Dutch visual artists, Oud was at first greatly admired by the advocates of the Modern style (such as Hitchcock) for his work as city architect of Rotterdam. However, when a few years afterward he patterned the façade of his design for the Shell headquarters building in The Hague in order to 'humanize' it, he was denounced and ostracized by his former associates for this 'regressive' move.[11] As it turned out, given the subsequent shift in fashion, if he had only waited twenty years, he might have been honoured as a Post-Modern pioneer.

Architects, like artists, are expected to be obsessed with their work. It is part of their romantic folklore. Their model is Michelangelo, who, when a friend expressed regret that he had never married and raised a family, replied, 'I have a wife too many already, namely this art'.[12] Such single-mindedness could be held to provide the motivation and dedication for the creative act, as well as to focus the intent and content of the work itself. None the less, the other face of obsessiveness is dogmatism and narrow-mindedness.

Consequently, even where the marketing aspects of eliminating the competition are discounted, the more virtuous belief of architects themselves that their work is unique because it portrays an absolute ideal, or results from invariable laws, or reveals the essential spirit of the age, or represents the very latest in aesthetic insights, equally guarantees the rejection of alternative viewpoints. Rather than welcoming the work of their creative colleagues, they more often reject it on the grounds that it is either outdated, inferior, or wrong.

What the architectural élite is left with is its own small preserve: the few isolated monuments deemed worthy of its own enjoyment. In this rarefied setting, the work of the genius is the only commodity recognized as art. Extended over time, this becomes the equivalent of an outmoded history of kings and queens (although, being traditionally a male-dominated profession, architecture has excluded women along with almost everyone else).

But the world of ordinary people is made up of countless buildings, not merely a few isolated monuments. The population of North America, for instance, has grown above a quarter of a billion persons in just a couple of hundred years. Most of these people live in cities on land that was recently open country. Vast numbers of buildings have been erected to accommodate them. This is the real story of architecture – the planning, design, construction, erection, and use of the buildings that make up our human environment.

Again, our current building needs include millions of homes, thousands of schools, hundreds of hospitals, billions of square feet of offices and stores (not to mention all the other building requirements of human life). These are not simple problems to be resolved easily. The architectural establishment is not set up to respond to the challenge due to its historical evolution. Its typical mode of operation has been to create unique solutions for a select few, which are then generalized by their followers for wider use. Architects naturally follow styles because they believe that styles embody the architectural truths of their time (if not eternity). But when combined with the rapid turnover of styles since the decline of centralized authorities, this has resulted in abrupt changes in ideas and images, as well as the idiosyncratic flourishes that accompany them.

Everyday buildings, under this regime, are conceptualized as cathedrals or factories or palaces. Their standard windows are conceived as leaded lights or glass walls or Palladian motifs. Their typical roofs take on turrets, or are hidden, or sprout cornices. Conversely, architects are unable to address the ordinary – but fundamental – concerns of their work in any systematic or consistent way. Preoccupied with the issue of styles (and their ideological rationalizations), they are unable as a profession to develop a coherent and progressive discipline.

What we have are random leaps of the imagination from individuals who extrapolate from their own limited circumstances and universalize their convictions. What we need are incremental improvements derived from the collective experience of the community. Buildings are more than cult objects for the initiated. They are in constant use and part of our daily lives. The aesthete's masterpiece must also accommodate its regular inhabitants.

In practice, neither benefits from the current system. Instead, both are subverted by the architectural profession. It is here that 'art' is turned into 'style,' a process that affronts the art world, leaves it with only the exceptional artwork to adulate, and causes the real world to be largely indifferent to its buildings.

The problem is one of ends and means. Architects are taught to believe that their work is of transcendental significance. This conceit has its roots in antiquity when they were functionaries of the state. It was cultivated during the Renaissance, when it was exploited by architects to elevate themselves above craftsmen. More recently, it has been used to defend their legitimacy as members of a profession and to distinguish them from engineers.

But architects are just as ordinary as the rest of the population. Nothing in their training or practice suggests that they have the resources to achieve their exalted aims. Far from giving them insights into metaphysical realms, architectural schools instruct students in the current architectural styles. If the school is 'good,' the apprentices' mentors are the inventors of their own aesthetic ideologies. If not, their teachers are themselves only intermediaries in the process of indoctrination. In either case, what students emerge with is a mode of design and an inflated sense of their own importance, acquired from the need to justify every design in terms of the profundity of its content.

This is not inevitable. Students could be taught to design buildings in a practical manner. They could be shown how buildings may be enhanced to give pleasure and interest to their use. These skills would be socially valuable. Instead, students are taught that the meanings they attribute to their designs are absolute and universal, and that buildings are simply a convenient medium provided by an acquiescent society for their artistic expression.

These are unrewarding qualities to take into the outside world and they seldom survive the transition. The evidence can be seen in the substantial difference between student projects and the design of actual buildings where the normal constraints of practice soon deflate the novice architect's pretentious claims to the level of everyday construction.

In the art-architecture credo favoured by architectural critics, the one sacrosanct element of design is the aesthetic component. But not too many building owners are willing to sacrifice economic and functional concerns to this metaphysical abstraction. In turn, few architects have the understanding or capability or single-mindedness to achieve it. In the process of accommodating all the components of a design, most architects find that practical considerations and common sense moderate their solution. Additionally, they usually have some regard for the people who use their buildings (not to mention those cases where the building's use requires that it should be attractive).

Architects therefore use the style they learned as just another factor in their design. It remains the overall organizing system, but only in vague general terms and only as far as it can be incorporated. The result is what we see in the streets. Basically workable buildings, touched up with the architectural fashions of the day, which, over the past two centuries, have included Neoclassicism, Neo-Greek, Italianate, Neo-Gothic, Second Empire, Neo-Romanesque, Arts and Crafts, Art Nouveau, Moderne, Modern, and Post-Modern, and their various divisions.

The results can range from the charming to the pompous, from the absurd to the brutal. Far from receiving any transcendental messages from them, all we get is a random assortment of vacuous images. To the 'experts,' such buildings are an insult to the dignity of art. Ironically, the same verdict of failure is conceded by the ordinary architects who perpetrate them. They may not be able to equal their idols, but their training ensures that they deplore the shortcomings of their colleagues (if not themselves).

At the height of the Modern style, and long before the subsequent verbal onslaught on it, British architects themselves condemned the prevailing level of design in a poll that showed that nine-tenths of them thought that it was indifferent or bad, and half of them believed it was the profession's own fault.[13] A decade later, a 1970s study of Manhattan architects showed that only a minority of them liked the work of even such widely known colleagues as Minoru Yamasaki and Edward D. Stone (whom critics had previously censured for being too decorative, that is, not profound).[14]

The paradox in these findings is that in the architects' world, the success of a style is the guarantee of its downfall. Art thrives on the unusual. Its spread, from its originators to its imitators, would ensure a limited time span even if its message were not distorted in the process. The art world is driven by new experiences and, once these

have become commonplace, it is eager to move on. But the filtering
down process that turns art into style also diffuses its assigned content as it passes through the hands of everyday practitioners, and
they recognize and regret its loss of significance.

In this context, style is the corruption of art, and a sign of its
aesthetic devaluation, a mark of its mediocrity in the eyes of the
profession that practises it. It is this inherent sense of failure that
haunts the profession and causes the lack of self-esteem that characterizes architects. To be even of the second rank in international
circles (and this includes the so-called best architects in many countries) is judged to be inferior.

Moreover, if most architecture is considered second-rate or less, it
is also secondhand or more. Given the attitudes of the profession,
architects normally adopt styles from wherever they appear, regardless of their place of origin. For example, the two most recent major
styles used in Canada have been imported from the United States by
Canadians studying at American universities: Modern from Harvard
under Walter Gropius; Post-Modern from Yale under Charles Moore.
The consequence is that buildings in Canada are dressed up in bor-
rowed styles largely unrelated to their physical or social environment.

Not too much can be expected of these local versions of international models. For styles not only embody a system of design, but
arise out of a particular set of circumstances. They therefore do not
travel well. Any modification from the original model to accommodate dissimilar local conditions usually compromises its symbolic
integrity. These conditions may range from a different climate to a
different way of life. Such variations can be seen in the characteristic
building qualities associated with northern and southern Europe, and
with the east and west coasts of North America. Consequently,
although buildings in any given style might be found anywhere
around the world, because of the way the architectural profession
functions, they are apt to be of an inferior standard. In other words,
provincial architecture is predisposed to be provincial.

It is also likely to be foreign. Because countries outside the art
world's generating centres are expected to adopt the styles it sanc-
tions, they are apt to end up with none of their own. This hardly
matters in those arts that are restricted mainly to museums. Visitors

expect to see the standard set of art-world icons, and most curators try to assemble a representative collection of them, regardless of which country their art galleries happen to be in.

But buildings are social artefacts and have a social significance beyond any art purposes their designers may profess. When architects imitate the internationally approved styles, their communities are left without the opportunity to develop their own symbols. This not only further reduces the capacity of architects to produce convincing designs (and justifies the critic's contempt for their work). It also means that the buildings people get are essentially irrelevant to their concerns. At worst, they might even parade undesirable qualities. Either way, they alienate the public from its own surroundings.

Broadly speaking, then, if the architectural élite despises most buildings, and the run-of-the-mill profession feels guilty about them, people generally may be described as largely indifferent. Having empowered the profession to act independently, the public has shown little interest in what the profession does. The public's opinion concerning the design of its buildings is difficult to ascertain, primarily because architects have so successfully excluded it from any involvement in their sphere of influence. A rare poll on architectural topics, taken in the late 1980s as a sequel to comments by Prince Charles, reported that more than half the respondents thought that modern buildings were an eyesore.[15] But there is other evidence to indicate that most people do not care for the designs that architects produce. In overall terms, the built environment is made up of two major components: houses that are manufactured for sale like other standard products, and other buildings erected with the direct involvement of architects. This division also marks the distance between professional and public taste. In a free market, people express their preferences through their purchases, and generations of professional cajoling have done little to make them like what the 'specialists' have to offer.

The result is that the homes people buy through real estate transactions, and the furnishings they choose, are conspicuously different from those that architects favour. The contrast may be seen in the magazines that cater to the two groups. A trade magazine that primarily serves the architectural profession, like *Architectural Record*, with a circulation of 77,000, supplies the current images (and key-words) that architects need to keep up-to-date. These are almost entirely in the architect's idiom. Nearly all the furnishings shown in the special issue of 'Record Houses 1990,' for instance, carefully fit the design of the buildings that contain them. In contrast, hardly a single piece of furniture illustrated in a 1990 article on 'creating beautiful interiors with retail furnishings' in a consumer magazine such as *House Beautiful* would be likely to appear in an architectural magazine. Here, the role of architects has been taken over by interior designers, who are closer in taste to a larger public represented by a magazine circulation eleven times as large.[16]

Perhaps providing the most telling commentary on the work of the architectural profession has been the remarkable spread of the conservation movement. Initially a reaction to the extensive razing of urban areas that occurred after World War II as the industrialized nations of the West renewed and expanded their physical resources, it soon became a philosophical ideal based on the proposition that a country's heritage was a spiritual asset. In the early years there were only limited protests against the destruction caused by expressways and urban renewal projects. By the mid-1960s, countries such as the United States were enacting laws to preserve existing buildings 'as a living part of our community life and development in order to give a sense of orientation to the American people.'[17]

Two factors in this new attitude have challenged the architects' traditional perception of their own authority. First of all, many of the buildings saved from destruction are the sort of familiar buildings that architects have been taught to disdain, but that are valued by the community as a whole. Nowadays whole districts of housing or ware-houses are protected that were never accepted into the architects' canon of significant monuments. Secondly, implicit in the new outlook is the assumption that today's architects are unable to support and (especially) to advance the aspirations of their public. From this per-spective, the purpose of conservation laws is not only to hold on to the past. It is also to prevent architects – and their employers – from ruining the future. Interestingly, many architects seem to have ac-cepted this conclusion by painstakingly incorporating pieces of old buildings in their designs, or attempting to make their new buildings look old (although they would doubtless give other reasons for doing so).

In its post–World War II phase, concern for the built environment was paralleled and encompassed by larger environmental concerns. It was also quickly outpaced by them. Brought to the public's notice in the early 1960s by Rachel Carson in *Silent Spring*, the ominous effects of pesticides were equalled by the devastation of nuclear fallout, industrial pollution, oil spills, acid rain, and other incipient catastrophes.[18] These provided a stirring backdrop to the growth of a worldwide environmental movement that has come to include not only citizen advocates but government agencies, political parties, and even its own philosophical discourse.[19]

That the impact of the human race on the natural environment has become a greater issue than the quality of its own constructed environment is obviously because the plight of the earth is seen as a more immediate and direct threat. It is also much easier to recognize. The result has been a fundamental shift in perception. An extreme illustration of this new sensitivity occurred in the 1970s when the United States Supreme Court halted the construction of a Tennessee Valley Authority dam to protect what was thought to be an endangered species of small fish.[20]

But in terms of the built environment, preservation is only one component of a solution. The natural environment has its own form, and experience has shown the difficulties and dangers of tampering with it. The form that the built environment has taken is a reflection of the human situation, which undergoes continuous change and, hopefully, in the long run, improvement. People are part of the existing natural environment; they alone are responsible for the ongoing creation of their own built environment.

It is this vision of what would be a better urban future than exists at present that is missing among people generally. Its absence leaves them open to continued exploitation by the architectural profession. There has been no public debate on the built environment equivalent to the one that has taken place over the natural environment. People are still silenced by their lack of knowledge. Without an understanding of their own objectives, they may prevent what they dislike, but they cannot achieve what they want.

There are major issues at stake here. The opposite to an exclusive, incomprehensible, irrelevant architecture, imposed from above, is a public, accessible, meaningful architecture, created out of community life. Buildings are well adapted to this role. They are ordinary artefacts in everyday use. They can provide an enjoyable setting for our daily routine. They can absorb and reflect our impulse to incorporate part of ourselves into the things we make and do. They can be used to express our realities, values, beliefs, and ideals. And they can give us a sense of who and what we are and where we live.

To realize these aims, we should be able to draw on the expertise of the architectural profession. But architects have made little effort to provide this service. They still look back to an authoritarian past, despite dramatic changes over the past two centuries. While many of them pay lip-service to the idea that design should respond to its social context, there is a considerable distance between what they say and what they do. Ultimately, their subject matter remains an outdated concept of art, not people, and their imagery is contrived, not rooted in social life. Nor has the profession tried to come to terms with its own deficiencies in any purposeful way. Engrossed by their own special interests, architects think their role is to proselytize their opinions, rather than enter into a discussion of their methods, values, and ambitions.

Formed over hundreds of years, these problems cannot be easily resolved. Architects are constrained by centuries of theory, history, and practice. Their attitudes are embedded in beliefs that stretch back to the beginnings of the profession. Caught up in their doctrine, which has become entrenched as architectural thought, it is easy for them to believe that the current situation is irreversible. But this is obviously false. They were active participants in creating the system and they can help change it. What is needed now is for the profession to be brought into line with the new social circumstances.

Here is where the solution lies. In democratic nations with an educated population, involvement in the formation of the built environment is no less a right and responsibility than participation in any other social issue. Architects function in the public domain, and receive their mandate to practise their profession through the laws approved by the community in which they work. In return, they should be held accountable for what they do.

To secure this new relationship, it will be necessary for architects to abandon obsolete myths. Architecture will have be redefined and grounded in a substantive theory that will provide a continuing basis for its practice. Its history and criticism must be redirected. The aims of architectural education must be reformulated. The responsibility of architects to the communities that delegate authority to them must be reasserted.

This cannot be done within the architects' prevailing structure of beliefs; the influence of bygone centuries is much too strong. We must unravel the past so that we can understand the present. If architecture is to become an effective and respected profession, a new framework of ideas is necessary to guide its future.

1.1 A city for three million inhabitants. Few of its buildings attract the approval of architectural experts. Few of its buildings reflect the character of its people. They lose both ways. The city could be anywhere in the world.

2 Myth and Architecture

*The profession has invented a series
of myths to protect and promote its
own interests.*

The architects' contention that their work possesses mystical qualities
dates back to ancient times when buildings were steeped in folklore
and religion. It was part of a process through which human beings
tried to come to terms with the enigma of life by endowing what
they thought or made with a transcendental reality of its own. How
blocks of stone or pieces of wood were actually elevated into potent
symbols is lost in obscurity. Perhaps a rock that served as an object
of worship was shaped to represent a god.[1] Or a structure erected to
shelter the cult statue assumed its own sacred character, in the same
way that the clothing of saints later became objects of veneration.
Certainly by the Roman era, even ordinary building elements had
been credited with occult powers to provide protection from malig-
nant spirits.[2] Two millennia later, the traces of these beliefs persist in
customs such as carrying brides over thresholds or gathering around
the family hearth.

When Vitruvius wrote the first existing treatise on architecture two
thousand years ago, it was taken for granted that the forms of the
temples had been received from the gods. Both the Doric and Ionic
Orders were named after mythical beings: Dorus, the son of the
nymph Phthia and Hellen, the eponymous ancestor of the Greek
nation; and Ion, his nephew, or perhaps even the son of Apollo, that
is, the grandson of the great god Zeus himself.[3] Such connections
guaranteed reverence and esteem for what in themselves were simply
buildings made out of ordinary materials.

This religious component was widened and strengthened by a

number of other symbolic connections. Building was linked to its
makers by the attribution of human traits to the Orders, and by the
depiction of human beings as a source of proportion and geometry
through the famous image of the outstretched body delineated by a
circle and a square.[4] This, in turn, tied both humankind and its structures to the cosmos through geometry and number. Harmony was to
be experienced in both the proportions of a temple and the music of
the celestial spheres. More generally, and in the long run more conse-
quentially, by declaring that architecture was founded on the eternal,
universal, and abstract laws of order, symmetry, and beauty, Vitruvius succeeded in divorcing building from the ordinary world and
elevating it into the metaphysical realm.

Passed down by Vitruvius, this Classical tradition was ultimately
to become the standard for the architectural world.[5] In later periods,
other styles were named in relation to it, either sympathetically if
they advanced its aims (for example, Renaissance and Neoclassicism,
or even Post-Modern Classicism) or pejoratively if they were in
opposition to it (for example, Gothic and Baroque). Architects, for
their part, still return to Vitruvius for the very definition of their
work, and continue to assume, as he stated, that it combines stability
and utility with beauty, or some other equally recondite quality.[6]

The Classical notion of beauty both externalized and secularized
what came to be considered the essential quality of art.[7] The establishment of a special aesthetic goal that was detached from religious
concerns, eventually removed the practice of art from its original
social base. Art was made rare, and its primary aesthetic component
was set outside and above the realm of everyday life. Beauty was
held to be a quality of things in the same way that it was manifested
in nature. But whereas the beauty of nature might be revealed to any
feeling person, the beauty of art was somehow only accessible to
uniquely endowed individuals or groups.

At first, this exclusiveness was not expressly embodied in the
theory. The proposition that human beings were part of a divine plan
also suggested that the capacity to perceive beauty must be innate in
all human beings; a gift that allowed us to rejoice in God's works
and, by extension, our own in his image. Or, later, the argument that
there was a concordance between the universe and humankind, so

that we and our art manifested the same underlying order or purpose or structure, implied that everyone should be able to respond to beauty (if not to create it themselves). How this interaction took place was open to debate. Some thought humans had a special aesthetic faculty; others believed it was a function of the soul; another possibility was that it was comprehended by the mind or through the senses or, in the case of the visual arts, directly by the eyes.

Regardless of the means, all such theories implicitly contained the corollary that the aesthetic experience was open to all human beings. If the qualities of beauty were objective, timeless, and universal, and the human race belonged to the same order of creation, then everyone should naturally respond to art if this was defined as the embodiment of beauty. Later connoisseurs, such as the nineteenth-century writer J.A. Symonds, claimed that this was true during the Renaissance, when every Italian was a judge of art, from the Pope on down to the clerk in a Florentine counting-house.[8] As most Florentines were probably poor or illiterate, and had little to do with art, this was no doubt an idealized view of the so-called golden age.[9] More accurately, it applied to a cultivated minority that deliberately accelerated the distancing of itself from the uncultivated majority.

In architecture, which was just about to be linked to the other visual arts, the move was part of its practitioners' ambition to raise their status in the social hierarchy. Historically having always served the church and the state, architects had operated as functionaries within the established system. This had brought them close to the centres of power, but seldom allowed them to have any power of their own outside the practice of their profession. Of course, there have been exceptions. Imhotep was not only chief architect when the Step Pyramid of Zoser was built in Egypt around 2700 B.C., but was also one of its leading state officials. In the twentieth century, Albert Speer was Adolf Hitler's arms production minister as well as his official architect.

Under the medieval guild system, however, architecture was still viewed as a craft, along with the other building trades.[10] This placed architects, or master masons as they were known, in an equivocal position. Because their long apprenticeship, which might extend for ten years, fully assimilated them and their work into the social order,

the clergy would often take credit for their designs. This was natural
where architecture was treated as part of the theological symbolism
of the times. As early as the fourth century, Eusebius of Caesarea had
equated the church entrance with the praise of God, flanked by the
light of Christ and the Holy Spirit.[11] Eight hundred years later, Abbot
Suger described the columns used in the construction of the choir of
S. Denis in terms of the twelve apostles surrounded by the minor
prophets.[12]

Architects could rise from even poor circumstances to sit at the
same table as their social superiors, whose cultivated manners they
had to learn to adopt. Observing that there was a better way to live,
they were, no doubt, motivated to improve their social standing.
They had good reasons. They were sometimes responsible for buildings of great importance. They had to solve complex functional
problems. They were expected to act with probity and competence in
the supervision and expenditure of large sums of money. And they
were able to create symbols that upheld and exalted the beliefs of
their influential masters. It was this aspect of their work that probably encouraged architects to indulge vicariously in the reflected
glory of the buildings they designed, which, in turn, increased their
own sense of worth and their ambition to be a recognized part of the
establishment they served.

The turning point in the achievement of this objective was an
incident involving the Renaissance architect, Filippo Brunelleschi.
Imprisoned while supervising the construction of his design for the
dome of Florence Cathedral, because he refused to pay his dues to
the stonemason's guild, he proved to be too valuable an individual
to the authorities to be treated in this way, and was quickly released
when they intervened and arrested one of his persecutors.[13] Of more
lasting importance, the theoretical justification for the elevation of the
architect's status was provided after Brunelleschi's death by his
younger contemporary and friend Leon Battista Alberti.

Educated in the classics and with a doctorate in canon law, Alberti,
the illegitimate son of a patrician Florentine, was instrumental in
incorporating architecture into the cultivated interests of the fifteenth-
century.[14] Like Vitruvius, whose treatise formed the model for his
own, Alberti attributed exceptional qualities to architects and their

work. But whereas Vitruvius glorified his own occupation as a professional architect, Alberti wrote with all the authority of a leading intellectual.

The same sort of arguments to be found in Vitruvius were now repeated and reinforced. Ordinary building craftsmen were no more than the mere instruments of architects, who conceived their designs in the realm of the mind and thereby subordinated practice to theory.[15] Derived from nature, discovered by reason, realized through geometry and proportion, their work embodied universal laws that only the ignorant or fools would question.[16] Looking at Alberti's design for the new front of S. Maria Novella in Florence, for instance, the ordinary viewer might merely have seen an odd façade added on to an old church. The *cognoscenti*, however, would have discerned that its outlines were based on the proportion of one to two, in musical terms an octave, which gave material expression to nature's intrinsic harmony.[17]

Stressing the great importance of architects' work, Alberti argued that it was only proper that they should seek employment by persons of the highest rank, who had the money and prestige necessary to advance their reputations.[18] In these circumstances, the effort to be accepted by the ruling class was largely unaffected by any accident of birth. The most famous example of this social mobility was the sixteenth-century architect, Andrea Palladio. A stonemason named Andrea di Pietro until the age of thirty, he was then adopted by the humanist Count Giangiorgio Trissino, who took him into his villa, educated him alongside young noblemen, and gave him the Classical name of Palladio. Three decades later, with his publication of *The Four Books of Architecture*, Palladio was to achieve lasting fame and have an unparalleled influence on European and North American architecture.[19]

The potency of the Vitruvian propositions on architecture had resulted from their combination of aesthetics and religion. This heady mixture was to continue, although the demands of Christian orthodoxy required some modification of the early connection of the Classical Orders with paganism. The convenient solution was to explain their origin in terms of functional development (based on wooden construction) rather than mythology, and to tie their design to the abstract, but sacred, cosmology that was the educated belief of the day.

The Christian God played a considerable role in this appeal to the transcendental importance of architecture. Alberti cited God for his number preferences; Palladio turned to God to justify the geometry of the circular church.[20] Even direct support from God was invoked when the Bible was added to the authors of antiquity, and the measurements set down for the Tabernacle in Exodus were taken as a revelational source of proportions.[21] There was no doubt in the minds of these architects as to the significance of what they did. Their designs were no less than microcosmic representations of the world created by God, and were a reflection of his existence.

Obviously, the persons who created such transcendental works had to have special qualities of their own. Usually not of noble birth, and often rising from humble circumstances, their talent had to be explained in terms other than upbringing and education. The notion of genius filled this need. Once again, God readily supplied the metaphor as the first architect, allowing the artist and especially the architect to be acclaimed as his surrogate.[22] 'Michael more than mortal/Angel divine,' wrote the Italian poet Ludovico Ariosto of Michelangelo, while his young friend Vasari rhapsodized over the genius of the man who had been sent down to earth by God to rescue the arts from the errors of the past.[23] A few centuries later, architects like Le Corbusier and Frank Lloyd Wright, supported by their acolytes, were still asserting their own claims to genius. Such extravagant claims became commonplace in the architectural world. God and nature; geometry, number, and proportion; truth and beauty; taste and genius: these became the architects' lexicon, rationalizing and glorifying their work in designing buildings for the powerful and the rich.[24]

This close relationship between architects and their employers became institutionalized in France under the absolute monarchy of Louis XIV. Urged on by Alberti and other Renaissance writers, French architects of the sixteenth century had sought to attain a similar status by distancing themselves from craftsmen and seeking equality with courtiers. While the process was furthered by Philibert Delorme, who was named architect to the king in 1548, its resolution came a century later when the royal administration took control of the profession as part of the centralization of the state.[25]

The immediate cause was the building of the east wing of the palace of the Louvre, designed initially by Louis Le Vau. The son of a master mason, he had succeeded in rising above his family's speculations in town houses for the *nouveaux riches* and designed the château of Vaux-le-Vicomte that was so magnificent that even Louis XIV was envious of it.[26] Le Vau's proposal for the Louvre was not impressive enough for the Sun-King's new minister, J.B. Colbert, who invited other architects to submit designs. When the celebrated Gianlorenzo Bernini's plan failed to consider the king's physical comfort, the project was returned to Le Vau, but this time as one member of a committee that included the architectural theorist, physician, and scientist Claude Perrault, and the king's painter, Charles Le Brun.

Six years had passed before the final design was approved, and Colbert seems to have concluded from this experience that it was time to organize the profession of architecture in a more structured way. The Académie Royale d'Architecture was set up in 1671 specifically to serve the interests of the king.[27] Appointed by the king, its members were not only responsible for advising him on the design of state buildings but also for establishing a theoretical basis for architecture that could be codified and taught. Both sides gained considerably from the transaction. Architects became a legitimate part of the royal establishment, which raised and ratified their status in society. This position was strengthened by their choice of a method of design that consolidated architecture as the arcane preserve of an initiated set.[28] Those who became adept at the authorized style were rewarded with an assured career. In return, architects assembled a set of architectural symbols that upheld and enhanced the power of the state. So powerful were these metaphors of superhuman scale, vast compositions, imposing symmetry, and inflexible order, that they lasted for more than two centuries and served not only the *ancien régime* and post-Revolutionary France, but also later democracies and dictatorships alike.

Founded on Classical principles and precedents, this codified architecture was detailed in lectures on theory that were given at the academy and disseminated through their publication, in a tradition started by its first director – and the school's first professor – François Blondel. For the next two centuries the school flourished with only minor changes. In spite of the upheavals of the revolution and Napoleon's reign – from which the school emerged in 1819 as the École des Beaux-Arts – a view of architecture and method of instruction evolved that had an enormous impact on the rest of the architectural world.

Based on the Orders, which were taken as archetypes from antiquity, and arranged in a systematic manner that gave them the appearance of being rational and objective, these printed courses compared the most outstanding authorities and advocated the best models to be followed. In doing so, the method itself brought the element of judgment into the aesthetic equation, and undermined the rigidity of the idea that beauty was an objective fact.

In architecture, the issue was part of the argument between the 'ancients' and the 'moderns.' Perrault rejected the unquestionable authority of antiquity concerning which proportions were the basis of beauty, and asserted the right to determine them through a reasoned analysis of precedents.[29] But if beauty was not to be experienced through a natural concordance of viewer and object and their mutual existence in an ordered universe, and if the aesthetic experience depended on some extra quality in the artist and some extra capability in the viewer, then how was this to be explained?

Early Renaissance writers, confronted with this problem, had admitted its impenetrability and invented an undefinable quality that was later described in French as a certain *je ne sais quoi*. In architectural terms, design was no longer to be based on absolute rules but would now have to depend on knowledge, reason, judgment, and taste. Conversely, the accessibility of art to the population at large was to be restricted to a small class of the enlightened and instructed. This was, of course, not new. An appreciation of art had long been deemed to be a desirable accomplishment of the perfect courtier.[30]

Under the French system, the nature of this cultivation was to be made explicit, so that it could be applied equally to both the profession and its supporters. Unlike in the general Western tradition, where the notions of genius and taste became separate (and often opposing) distinguishing features of the stereotypical artist and critic, in French architectural theory genius was made subject to taste, which was derived from knowledge and reason. Design decisions were to depend neither on rules nor on inspiration, but on an orderly analysis of the problem, a clear understanding of precedents, a close study of possible alternatives, and a judicious sense of fitness: in other words, an educated taste.

The contention that only cultivated persons could appreciate beauty appeared frequently in the works of eighteenth-century writers, and was ultimately incorporated into a moral critique of capitalism, where ugliness was equated with a philistine middle class.[31] In the meantime, the claim to a superior taste simply confirmed the existing division of society into the educated few and the illiterate mass. This attitude was supported by the argument that only the leisured class was sufficiently detached from the necessities of life to make judgments on purely aesthetic grounds. Interestingly, philosophers argued their case from mutually exclusive positions, demanding a return to innocence and nature (or in architecture, its equivalent, the buildings of antiquity), and assuming that a sophisticated knowledge of the past was necessary to make informed judgments.

The effect of this emphasis on taste was to allow an element of personal interpretation and innovation within the Classical tradition itself. Carried further, it enabled aesthetic activists to advocate their own preferences. For the world outside, it led ultimately towards a sociology of art.

By the mid-eighteenth century, philosophers such as David Hume were attempting to explain why, if taste was based on universal principles, there were so few connoisseurs, and coming to the conclusion that personal and social factors intervened.[32] These might be occasioned by individual prejudices or group preferences, such as the young liking amorous subjects while the old favoured philosophical writings. Or they might reflect the beliefs and attitudes of whole periods or nations, which could be moulded by different conditions. None the less, it was still generally assumed that although beauty might be difficult to recognize, it actually existed in some form or another.

But while intellectuals struggled to understand whether beauty was

absolute or relative, the issue itself was rendered less important by
changing concerns within the visual arts themselves. For by the end
of the century, the traditional ideal of beauty had been supplemented
by two other aesthetic interests, the sublime and the picturesque.[33]

The translation into French of the Greek treatise 'On the Sublime'
in rhetoric by Longinus, which also fostered the notion of genius,
had diverted attention from the rules that poetry followed to the
emotions it aroused. The same aesthetic quality was soon to be found
in nature and in art. The gentry on their grand tours learned to look
with awe and reverence at the vastness of the sea and the majesty of
the Alps, while the sight of ruins conjured up visions of a noble past.
In buildings, this quality of the sublime was to be achieved through
extended perspectives, vast gloomy interiors, and an inflated scale (as
in Napoleon's Arc de Triomphe in Paris, which is more than three
times taller than its Roman counterpart).[34]

This new ingredient split the problem of how art might be recognized into object and subject, cause and effect. If, as its advocates
claimed, there were features in art that stirred the (sensitive) soul but
were not especially beautiful in themselves, then it could be argued
that the aesthetic event was a relational experience rather than the
reaction (no matter how imperfect or biased) to a transcendental
ideal. Generalized as a scientific proposition, this contention – that
certain characteristics and arrangements of form evoked particular
human feelings or associations – provided a theoretical motivation
for the nineteenth-century interest in an experimental psychology of
art. Subsequently, it led also to the idea that design can affect behaviour, a lingering belief among architects that in recent times has been
used as one more argument to convince outsiders of the importance
of the profession.

Similarly, eighteenth-century architects discovered the virtues of
the picturesque – an interest in variety and dramatic effects that first
appeared in landscape painting, manifested itself in ruins, and ultimately contributed to the revival of the Gothic style. The rediscovery
of the Gothic heritage also supported the emerging ideas that connected art with society, and gave architecture yet another metaphysical rationalization.

Writing in the early decades of the eighteenth century, the Italian philosopher, Giambattista Vico, had argued that societies produced their own institutions, and that these were infused by a similar outlook that was conditioned by its time and place.[35] Vico's works were either unknown or ignored by his contemporaries, yet by the end of the century, the notion that there was an overriding genius that permeated the activities of nations and/or eras had been assimilated into intellectual thought.

The incipient awareness that different times and places produced different architectural styles had already led the Baroque architect, J.B. Fischer von Erlach, to include examples of buildings from the Middle and Far East in his historical survey of 1721.[36] Some of these exotic buildings were soon to be seen in person by architects like William Chambers, who travelled to the Orient while working for the Swedish East India Company, and not only published drawings of Chinese buildings, but also designed his own pagoda for the Royal Botanic Gardens at Kew.[37] By the end of the eighteenth century, this knowledge was generally available to practising architects, for example, George Dance, who mixed Indian with medieval motifs in his design for the new façade of London's Guildhall.[38]

The reawakened interest in Gothic had a more immediate and lasting impact on both architectural theory and practice. Signalled in England in the mid eighteenth century by Horace Walpole, who helped redirect the cultivated taste of the period by renovating and enlarging his house at Strawberry Hill, Twickenham, in a Gothic idiom, it was heralded in Germany by J.W. von Goethe.[39] This new awareness of the Gothic era accelerated the fundamental shift in the aesthetic outlook of the day. By leading to the recognition that Classical architecture was not unique, and that Gothic architecture could not be judged by Classical standards, it ultimately reduced the Classical tradition to just one of two equal, if different, styles, each with its own particular characteristics.

It could be argued further that this division of two historical periods mirrored the human condition itself with its duality of contending but complementary facets of mind and emotion, reason and faith. Classical architecture, the reasoning went, embodied the same timeless laws that underlay and gave rise to the harmony of the universe. According to the trend-setting Walpole, one needed only one's passions to respond to Gothic architecture, whose very stones seemed to be imbued with numinous qualities that stirred the imagination and transfused the soul.[40]

It is not surprising that, looking backwards to earlier centuries, the writers of the time should have assumed that these very different value systems preceded and informed the architectural products that were associated with them. Each had deeply influenced the history of the West; each had produced buildings of very different design; each was more or less specific to a given time; each seemed to be characteristic of a different place – with the Classical being attributed to the Mediterranean area, and the Gothic to northern Europe. What can be termed the *Zeitgeist* or spirit-of-the-age theory of art was rapidly incorporated into architectural history and theory.[41] If architecture was affected by social conditions, then it was a simple, if illogical, step to reverse the equation and to claim that architecture was a symbol of them. This was given credibility by the historical relationship between the major monuments of architecture and the church and the state, where the buildings represented the interests of the ruling establishment, which in turn, was taken to represent society as a whole.

Popularized by Goethe and other German writers, the notion of the spirit of the age had already reached its final form by the early years of the nineteenth century, when an anonymous writer claimed that architecture commemorated the genius of the people of every nation and age, and served as an index to their minds and a key to their histories.[42] The idea was used, unsuccessfully, as a goad by critics of historical revivalism in their attempt to inaugurate a uniquely nineteenth-century style. More important, it became the organizational principle of architectural history.

The linkage between the character of a nation or an era and its art was made by the German archaeologist, J.J. Winckelmann, generally considered to be the first modern art historian. This initial move had important consequences when architecture was assimilated into the new discipline. It led to the art aspects of architecture being overemphasized to the detriment of its social and practical considerations, which caused buildings to be viewed as architectural art rather than as social artefacts. This, in turn, obscured and distorted the real connection between a society and its buildings.

The linkage also had a more academic legacy. By the mid-twentieth century, even a distinguished art historian like Ernst Gombrich could adopt its simplistic formula and, in his standard text, *The Story of Art*, equate Neoclassical architecture with 'The Age of Reason,' ignoring the reality that the period not only included individuals of his own intellectual bent, but also witnessed various wars as well as the squalid and brutal conditions under which the majority of people were forced to live.[43] Furthermore, in treating art as if it had its own objective existence, and not questioning its relationship to society at large, art historians greatly reinforced its acquired legitimacy, and themselves became major participants in the self-perpetuating activities of what could now be termed the art world.

Meanwhile, the historical approach to design based on places and times other than the Classical had other results. For talented architects like Dance, it was an incentive to disclaim rules, for which he denied any demonstrable evidence, and to rely on personal genius. For run-of-the-mill architects, it gave licence to produce the Egyptian prisons or Doric fish markets that the early nineteenth-century architectural polemicist A.W.N. Pugin mocked.[44] For the advocates of the Gothic Revival, it was the signal to substitute the virtue of truth for the ideal of beauty, which was so reduced in value among the initiated as ultimately to become a term with embarrassing or even disparaging overtones. Infused with moral fervour by Pugin and the prominent Victorian aesthete John Ruskin, the example of the Gothic led to the call for the honest use of materials and the truthful expression of the structure, in direct opposition to the practice of Neoclassical architects and their earlier defence of the architectural mystique.

The architects of the Gothic Revival, appropriating the position once held by Neoclassical architects, turned again to God to validate their arguments. In this vein, Ruskin wrote in his introduction to *The Seven Lamps of Architecture*, 'There is nothing so small but that we may honour God by asking His guidance of it.'[45] But if God was still the preferred authority for some architectural writers as testimony for the truth of their theories, the same demands of taste could also be couched in more rationalistic terms where timely.

This was done by the French medievalist E.E. Viollet-le-Duc, who invoked practical common sense to explain the merits of Gothic

architecture, even though his reasoning led him to dismiss the architectural achievements of the previous two hundred years.[46] Extrapolating from the Gothic example, he argued that the logic of solving
contemporary problems with modern materials and techniques
would not only lead to good design but also ensure that buildings
expressed the characteristics of their age.

Nineteenth-century critics had persistently called for an architectural style that would be expressive of its era.[47] At the same time, they
had been unable to suggest what it might look like. Existing visual
tastes were too entrenched to allow a new style to emerge from the
spirit-of-the-age theory, even when confronted by the utilitarian buildings of the day. Nor was the situation advanced by Viollet-le-Duc's
own images of masonry buildings incorporating odd-looking iron
supports.

Moreover, in France, the prestige and power of the École des
Beaux-Arts formed a considerable obstacle to change (or, as it was
viewed, heresy). This was dramatically illustrated when Napoleon
III's appointment of Viollet-le-Duc as its professor of history in 1863
was rejected by the students, who shouted him down when he attempted to lecture.[48] Forced to resign, he communicated his ideas
through his published discourses, which greatly influenced other
architects around the world.

If the French were not yet ready to give up the security of the
Classical tradition, conditions in Britain were more conducive, and
even instrumental, to an adjustment of the existing situation. There
were a number of reasons for this adjustment both inside and outside
the world of architecture.

Triggered by the idea of progress that had thrived with the rise of
science, originality had become a desired quality in art, ultimately to
be incorporated in the notion of the avant-garde.[49] As with today,
originality in art did not necessarily mean some sort of linear progress, but was solely the expression of a new aesthetic outlook that
could result even from reworking a past style, such as Egyptian
Revival or Italianate (or, more currently, Art Deco).

Although now firmly linked with the other visual arts that came
to be conceived and developed in a more personal way, architecture
remained ostensibly rooted in more objective conditions. Neverthe-

less, it too was caught up in the same preoccupations and was similarly (if until recently, more slowly) affected by changing fashions. To some extent, this was due to the relationship between producer and purchaser. Painters had already supplemented direct commissions by taking the chance of selling their own creations in the marketplace. Until the nineteenth century, architects had remained generally under the patronage of the ruling circle, and were required to share their enthusiasms with it. The architects who were instructed by the guilds, or taught in the academies, or fashioned by the state building administrations, or tempered by association with patrons like the Farnese, were well fitted to serve those who employed their skills. These architects had striven for, and largely achieved, a recognized place in the ruling establishment, whereby they tacitly accepted the governing standards of the day. Consequently they and their employers generally concurred as to the validity and merit of the style in which they worked.

This equilibrium foundered with the acceleration of capitalism in the nineteenth century. Several trends in Britain initiated the new era. The concentration of the population (which quadrupled during the period) in towns and cities, the proliferation of building needs and types, the growing influence of merchants and industrialists and their presence on building committees, as well as the emergence of other building disciplines such as quantity surveyors, engineers, building contractors – these broke the intimate connection between architects and their traditional employers.

Architects found themselves in an equivocal position in this new relationship. Caught up in the division of labour that accompanied industrialization, they now began to organize themselves into an independent profession that was required to sell its services on the open market. But although they might belong to the same social stratum as their employers, they did not necessarily share the same taste. John Soane, for example, who was considered a model of the new professional architect, had risen from a working-class family to become the professor of architecture at the Royal Academy and was knighted at the end of his life. But as an expert in his field, he felt obliged to denounce the parsimony and bad taste of even aristocratic employers, which smothered the artist's 'finer feelings.'[50]

In the years ahead, both architects and their employers (now euph-
emistically called clients, following the precedent of other professions
in recasting the relationship between the payer and the payee[51]) were
to come increasingly from the middle class.[52] What they had in common was a mode of life; what separated them was the architects'
specialized training. It set them apart not only from entrepreneurs
(from whom they gradually dissociated themselves for social, professional and aesthetic reasons), but also from the gentry, who otherwise shared their values and manners.

These radically new conditions introduced conflicts in the manner
in which architecture was conceived and practised. In one way, they
encouraged the proliferation of styles that might catch the notice of
potential employers and bring fame and commissions to their originators, thereby undermining the claim that there were acknowledged
principles of design. But architects were also deeply conscious of the
need to protect the significance of their work, which, without justification, was little different from the builder's trade. Shorn of its historical alliance with the state and the church, which had been the
major foundation of its claim to metaphysical significance, architecture was now left with only the support of aesthetics to defend its
alleged importance.

As it turned out, this was no inconsiderable heritage. The impact
on the world at large of the idea that aesthetics was important, was
more pervasive than might have been expected. To a large extent,
aesthetics had come to be the property of an educated section of the
population, which had invested a considerable amount of its own
reputation in the presumption of the authenticity of the notion of
good taste. It was certainly not ready to give up, or even question
seriously, a concept that had long marked the division between itself
and those it regarded as its inferiors.

The aesthetic doctrine was therefore assimilated into the broader
currents of society that the educated class came to control. Incorporated into public education, it became a component of the academic
image of what constitutes a cultivated person. Put forward as a
measure of a cultured nation, it continues to be an admired ideal.[53]
The fact that many of its supporters do not themselves participate in

art establishment activities, yet feel that they and others ought to, underlines the power of ideas produced by centuries of intellectual discourse.

This reached a crescendo in the twentieth century with a whole industry of practitioners, art historians, and critics engaged in legitimating their product by fabricating its own history, theory, myths, literature, records, monuments, and heroes. Produced in overwhelming detail, this output gave an almost objective reality to a practice that had earlier been only the experiential property of a very small, if powerful, group.

That even supposedly level-headed scientists were not immune to the unproved assumption that art had an objective existence of its own, became evident when aesthetics itself was adopted as a branch of psychology. For where scientists might have been hesitant to search for the physiological properties that determined religious preferences, they did not seem to have doubted that there must be some biological basis for the judgments that had been evolved in the world of art.

Investigating the question of proportion in the 1870s – long after it had lost its primary interest for artists and even architects – early experimenters like the physicist G.T. Fechner sought verification of the efficacy of the golden section (the divine proportion of the Renaissance), with questionable success.[54] Subsequent experiments have fallen between two poles. They have been either so limited in their scope as to produce results that are almost trivial in aesthetic terms, or they have attempted to deal with the total phenomenon of art and have failed to arrive at any convincing explanations. The real failure of experimental aesthetics, however, has been to find answers that relate to the human species as a whole.[55]

This problem was to some extent addressed by the eminent mathematician G.D. Birkhoff in the 1920s.[56] Birkhoff proposed a quantifiable aesthetic measure M that would be equal to O (for order, corresponding to a positive tone of feeling gained from associations) divided by C (for complexity, corresponding to tension due to what he termed automatic motor adjustments). This equation was based on the long-standing speculation that beauty resulted from some combination of the qualities of unity and diversity within an object.

In his study of the musical quality of poetry, Birkhoff compared Shakespeare's sonnets with nursery rhymes and hymns, thereby allowing the possibility of a valid aesthetic experience outside the realm of traditional art. Yet Birkhoff too believed that such experiments should be conducted with subjects who were knowledgeable of the art form under investigation, that is, who were already conditioned in their judgments.[57] The same specious reasoning was supported by the noted psychologist H.J. Eysenck, who saw nothing wrong in the proposition that the taste of art students was superior to that of students of dental technology, because they agreed with the judgments of art 'experts.'[58] In following Eysenck's hypothesis that there was some underlying property of the nervous system that determined our aesthetic judgments, other writers similarly continued to use art-world interests as their standard, apparently with no awareness of the vagaries of art history, and simply ignored the difference between biological responses and sociological norms.[59]

Although scientific research itself had little impact on architectural design, the scientific method (or its semblance) came to be adopted by architects as an influential metaphor. Part of the nineteenth-century case for an architecture that responded to contemporary conditions was its comparison with the obvious advances of engineering and technology. Writing in the 1840s, the American sculptor Horatio Greenough had not only used nature as the traditional model for art but also marked the progress between the ancient galley and the latest frigate, and suggested that architecture would be improved by following the same methodology. Buildings that satisfy ordinary needs, observed Greenough, might well be called 'machines.'[60]

His compatriot, the architect Louis Sullivan, preferred to continue to look to nature for his guidance. Determined to formulate his own single, universal principle of design, Sullivan adopted the theory from natural history that function and form were interrelated, and turned it into an architectural credo. Not that Sullivan's approach to functionalism derived from practical considerations, which are usually ascribed to his uncelebrated partner, Dankmar Adler. Expressed through poetic comparisons with 'the sweeping eagle in his flight or the open apple-blossom,' Sullivan's notion of functionalism was just as much a mystical invention (and glorification of ordinary building design) as the image of the Orders that had sustained the Classical tradition, and added a further device to the arsenal of architectural polemics.[61] Reduced to the axiom that 'form ever follows function,' this glorification of the utilitarian components of Vitruvius' famous triadic definition of architecture (in seventeenth-century parlance, 'Commoditie, Firmenes, and Delight'), provided yet another dimension to its ostensible significance, and brought architectural metaphysics into the twentieth century.[62]

If the advocates of a Modern style defined functionalism in more prosaic terms, they also extended its scope and meaning to include not only practical considerations of plan and structure, but also the psychological and sociological needs of their inhabitants (or 'users,' as architects came to call them), and, ultimately, their spiritual welfare.[63] The social reformer Robert Owen, in the 1800s, had promoted his plan for model villages on the principle that man's 'character is formed *for* and not *by*' him, and in the belief that they would make people more civilized.[64] Architects of the Modern style similarly contended that the plain surfaces and large glass areas they designed for buildings such as sanatoriums, open-air schools, or houses like Richard Neutra's Health House in Los Angeles, would have a salutary effect on their occupants. Van Eyck, for example, claimed that his design for a children's home in Amsterdam would untwist twisted children through the healing powers of its form and space.[65]

Architects relied on their intuitive faith in these matters, although Neutra looked forward to the day when they would be supported by scientific knowledge.[66] The impetus towards this occurred during World War II when investigations into the lighting, colour, and other conditions affecting factory production brought scientists into the study of architectural design.[67] Their research took two directions. One has tried to discover which architectural elements people respond to; the other has endeavoured to show how those elements affect people's behaviour. Both have been methodologically suspect, with the same sort of problems that marked the psychology of aesthetics, and scientists themselves have drawn back from earlier assumptions that the interaction between design and behaviour is a simple matter of stimulus and response.[68]

Besides, for most architects, the information received from scientists has been either too general to add much to their common experience, or too specific to be readily applicable in other circumstances.[69] The architectural profession has also ignored the attempt by scientists to invade its aesthetic territory with prescriptions of what its design choices should be. At the same time, the belief that design affects human behaviour continued to influence the way architects considered and justified their choices. This belief peaked with their endorsement of Le Corbusier's vision that his radiant city plan would usher in a better way of life, a claim that raised architects, at least in their own eyes, to the powerful position of social engineers.[70]

The extraordinary achievement of Le Corbusier was to combine all these transcendental propositions into a convincing fiction, and to attach them to the image of his own architectural style. Following his arrival on the avant-garde scene in Paris in 1916, Le Corbusier dominated the architectural world until well beyond his death in 1965. In his own forty or so books, and the countless more written by his devotees, the advocacy of his work incorporated almost every previous architectural rationalization.[71]

These made up an impressive list. On one side were the traditional assertions that architecture (such as the ancient Greek and his own) represented a parallel world of human creation that embodied the same laws as those manifested in the timeless universe. These laws were denoted by ratio and geometry, as in the Classical tradition. Le Corbusier's updated version of symmetry, called the modulor, comprised a set of proportions derived from the Fibonacci series and (once again) the golden section, based – with poetic licence and possibly wit – on the height of a stereotypical Englishman.[72] By that time, however, the architectural metaphor had passed from the world of Newton to the space-time image suggested by Einstein.

Of more originality was Le Corbusier's brilliant merging of earlier aesthetic and social theories of art. Here the machine (or at least its idealization) took a central role, being treated as a manifestation of the same order of logic as that found in nature, as well as the symbol of the spirit of the age. This fusion of ideas dealt decisively (if, as events proved, only temporarily) with the issue of what constituted a legitimate style, by contending that it was both contemporary and timeless.

Moreover, transferred to his designs, Le Corbusier's explanatory text that the house was 'a machine for living in,' also suggested the inevitability of his painted cubic forms, and conciliated those advocates of functionalism who were the heirs of the various ethical prohibitions and materialistic demands of earlier theories.

Finally, by extending this aesthetic discourse to the design of entire cities, Le Corbusier led the architectural profession to believe that its role was not just to design individual buildings but to plan society as a whole, and significantly inflated its perception of its own importance. Imbued with the notion that their work would be instrumental in creating a utopian future, architects were once again convinced that they were at the centre of events.

In this, they were encouraged by the injection of Marxist ideas about the relationship of art to the prevailing economic structure. Karl Marx himself, with a taste for Classicism, had pondered whether artistic ideals might be autonomous. Nineteenth-century aesthetic reformers had insisted, however, that architecture and society were inextricably linked. In its assertion that the general character of the spiritual processes of life was determined by material causes, the Marxist position was very close to architectural interests of the time. It reaffirmed the earlier proposition that some predominant 'spirit' of social life conditioned others that were less primary, and provided later architects with the key to defining this relationship.

Certainly, the advent of the Modern style was an intoxicating time for architects. 'The destiny of architecture is to express the orientation of the age,' proclaimed its proponents after setting up in 1928 their organization, the Congrès Internationaux d'Architecture Moderne (CIAM).[73] The age did not seem too interested at the time. Economic depression, dictatorships, and war, not to mention considerable professional dislike of the new style, restricted its spread until after World War II. Its success came only when victory over the Nazi regime brought people to associate Neoclassicism with regression and to link the Modern style with a more enlightened era.

The massive rebuilding program that followed the end of the war spread Modern architecture across the non-Communist world. Unlike in painting, whose prewar luminary, Pablo Picasso, was quickly superseded by abstract expressionists and other avant-garde artists, the leaders of the Modern movement largely succeeded themselves. The reason was not the lack of compelling alternatives, but that, given the underlying belief that there was only one valid style for the period, alternatives were rejected as unnecessary heresies.

These last few monuments of the Modern masters, who were by then more than sixty years of age, were overwhelmed by the mass of buildings erected in the Modern style. Shorn of its metaphysical associations, what remained not only appeared trivial but often looked crude, ugly, and oppressive. For a generation of architects brought up on the visionary fare of Le Corbusier and others, it was once again necessary to reinvent the heroic qualities architecture had lost. The remedy was to surface in the work and words of the American, Louis Kahn, who took over as the spiritual leader of the profession in the decade before his death in 1974.

Of the same age as the principal architects of the second rank of the Modern style in the 1930s – Berthold Lubetkin in Britain, Alberto Sartoris in Italy, José Luis Sert in Spain – Kahn saw his reputation burgeon in the 1960s as that of his previously better-known contemporaries declined. By 1962, when he gave the annual discourse at the Royal Institute of British Architects in London, the police had to be called in to control the crowds that were turned away.[74] For his many disciples, the philosophy of design that he advocated as a professor at Yale and the University of Pennsylvania, once again returned architecture to the level of profound significance from which it had fallen. Merging Jungian and Classical notions of form within a quasi-religious ontological framework buttressed by analogies with nature and joined to some rudimentary sociology, Kahn added yet another chapter to the metaphysical aggrandizement of an occupation that might otherwise be viewed by outsiders as a technical skill.[75]

Such inspirational ideas expressed poetically, as in the story of the priestess who saw God in her house, deeply affected the younger generation of architects.[76] In Europe, the result was a shift in their metaphysical ground, while the Modern style remained relatively intact. But in the United States, more radical architects took the opportunity to free themselves from its constraints. Professing to be

disillusioned by the practical failures of the visionary edifice constructed by their elders, they proceeded to demolish it, substituting
their own different, if equally questionable, contentions. The old
avant-garde of the Modern movement had claimed that it acted –
however perversely – for the public good. The new avant-garde
simply revelled in the creativity of its art.

Although it was initially tied to the proposition that artists were
the vanguard of social change, the concept of the avant-garde that
had emerged from the nineteenth century had two different roots.[77]
One was the value placed on originality, which had come to be a
major incentive and contributed to the demand for artistic freedom
from the conservatism and control of the academies. The other was
the notion of the spirit of the age. For if art reflected the spirit of
society, then who was better fitted to recognize and reveal its purpose than artists – an inference that led the activists of the Soviet
wing of the Modern movement to contend that they had foretold the
Russian Revolution.[78] In either case, given the indifference, or even
hostility, of society at large, the outcome was the image of the alienated artist who adopted the mantle of repudiated genius.

In the real world, however, rejecting society could have serious
consequences. While it might be feasible for painters, who took their
chances in the marketplace with their finished art products, architects, who needed clients to pay for their work and were generally
more intent on maintaining their professional and business status,
were less inclined to be so rash.

The early protagonists of Modern architecture had experienced
both situations. Initially, they had been closely tied to avant-garde art
movements, so that expressionism, cubism, futurism, constructivism,
neoplasticism and purism all had their architectural counterparts. It
was this image of the alienated artist, stemming from the episode of
the nineteenth-century Impressionists, that coloured Le Corbusier's
later summing up of his life with the comment that 'Some men have
original ideas and are kicked on the behind for their pains.'[79]

The initial success of the Modern style as a movement in the
interwar years altered the situation for its participants. Instead of
being depicted as avant-garde art, the new architecture could more
expediently be promoted as the legitimate and logical style of its era.

Under this rubric, architects were able to present themselves as the guardians of an objectively valid architecture with the social mission to ensure its adoption.

The new avant-garde could discard this position because it was no longer necessary. The post-World War II growth of an educated, affluent middle class, led by a sophisticated advertising industry, and intent on acquisition, almost guaranteed a receptive market for the purveyors of art, which had come to be treated as just another consumer product.

The two outlooks were well illustrated by the altercation over the 1979 competition for the Portland Building in Oregon, which was won by Michael Graves. To the spokesmen for the Moderns, the design was unprincipled, nothing more than 'an enlarged jukebox,' more suited to Las Vegas than a respectable city. The response of the Post-Moderns was to condemn their elders for being 'boring.'[80]

Freed from the need to find collective legitimacy in a utopian world-view, imagination now flourished at an unprecedented level, in both the imagery produced and its verbal rationalizations. The Portland Building provided a typical example, its facade being eulogized by one writer for the 'explosive force of the gigantic pilasters, with their rushing flutes rising out of darkness ... like energy emitted from the capitals, blasting the keystone from civilization's arch, irradiating alike the iconic human body and his mythic shelter.'[81]

This is the rhetoric of art, and it seems fitting that a number of the key Post-Modern buildings of recent decades have been art galleries. Nor is it surprising that architecture has taken this direction when the cost of a building such as the Wexner Center for the Visual Arts in Columbus, Ohio, designed by Peter Eisenman and completed in 1989, was less than the corresponding price of a Picasso self-portrait.[82] For art today is not a freak commodity but a potentially valuable business investment.

In exchange, architects can offer works that are visually diverting, or interesting within the history and conventions of architectural aesthetics, or that stand as metaphorical commentaries on various aspects of the meaning of life. Given the absorption of art into a free-market economy, architects need no longer profess social relevance as a necessary qualification for their justification. All that currently matters is that a design should be a media success.

But regardless of the particular differences between various styles, the only real change has been in image-making rather than substance. The essential characteristics of the art world still persist. It remains a self-indulgent activity for a very small minority. It continues to justify its practices by the pretensions of its claims. It doggedly holds on to the myth that it is the only authoritative producer of culture for society as a whole. And it continues its long-standing tradition of ignoring, deriding or excluding everybody else who does not share its interests.

If the only result of these actions was to enrich the lives of the individuals involved, we might well admire and applaud their achievements. Unfortunately, their example and influence have left the architectural profession as a group of confused and misguided would-be specialists, doing more harm than good, not only to themselves, but to the communities they are supposed to serve.

2.1 Architects create complex myths to explain their work. In the distant past, typical sets of columns and beams were glorified as Orders, and their origins attributed to the legendary ancestors of the Greeks. The Ionic Order was said to stand for the ideal of female beauty.

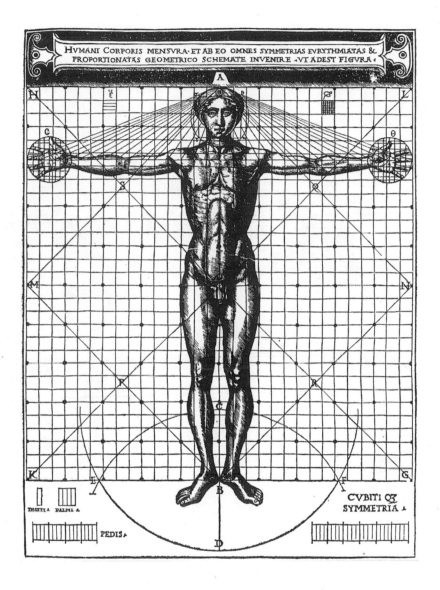

2.2 Similarly, the ordinary geometry and measurements that architects used were linked to the size and proportions of the male body, which supposedly embodied the underlying structure of the universe.

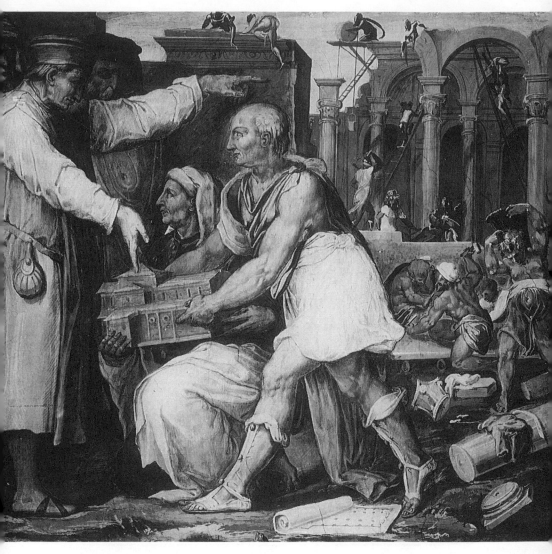

2.3 In the same way that buildings acquired significance through the events that took place in them, architects gained vicarious prestige from their powerful employers. In this painting by Giorgio Vasari, the fifteenth-century architect Filippo Brunelleschi, accompanied by the sculptor Lorenzo Ghiberti, is seen presenting the model of the church of S. Lorenzo to his patron, Cosimo de Medici.

2.4 Later architects further developed their own image. In the sixteenth century, Philibert Delorme depicted the architect as a man of learning, advancing towards a palm tree that symbolized his glory.

2.5 The *cognoscenti* insisted that architecture disclosed transcendental truths. For them, Leon Battista Alberti's new Renaissance façade for the medieval church of S. Maria Novella in Florence did not simply offer visual pleasure, but was a manifestation of nature's immutable laws.

2.7 The image of genius. Michelangelo, supporting Christ, in his Florence Pietà.

2.6 The idea of God as the first architect provided the ultimate authority. The reference was to the Wisdom of Solomon, where God was proclaimed to have ordered all things by measure and number and weight.

2.8 The difficulty experienced in obtaining a new east front for the palace of the Louvre that would sufficiently reflect the dignity of the 'sun king' Louis XIV, prompted the establishment of a royal academy of architecture. Its school developed a style that glorified the state through elementary geometry, exaggerated scale, and inflexible order.

2.9 This symbolism of power became the architect's international trademark. The Royal Palace in Madrid, Spain, was designed for the French-born king Philip V, by an Italian architect, G.B. Sacchetti, in 1738.

2.10 The rise of capitalism altered the relationship between architects and their employers. Architects in the English-speaking world became part of the free enterprise system and were forced to offer their services in the open market like other entrepreneurs. The resulting free-for-all could lead to the type of opportunist caricatured as Pecksniff by Charles Dickens.

2.11 The more dignified and ultimately rewarding strategy for architects was to organize as a group to protect their status and sphere of activity. Draped in a Roman toga, the bust of John Soane that Francis Chantrey made in 1829 portrayed the image of the high-principled professional.

2.12 The architects of the Gothic Revival movement of the nineteenth century substituted truth for beauty as their professional ideal, but what they meant by that is not readily apparent in buildings such as the S. Pancras Hotel by George Gilbert Scott.

2.14 Technology provided other metaphors. The machine served two purposes. It represented the era of industrialization, and acted as a symbol of universal logic. This potent fusion of traditional cosmology with the idea that architecture expresses the spirit of the age was given its definitive image by Le Corbusier in the twentieth century. His vision of the Contemporary City convinced architects that their appointed role was to plan the world.

IF WE CANNOT YET — RECONCILE ALL OPINIONS,

LET US ENDEAVOUR — TO UNITE ALL HEARTS.

IT IS OF ALL TRUTHS THE MOST IMPORTANT, THAT THE CHARACTER OF MAN IS FORMED FOR—NOT BY HIMSELF.

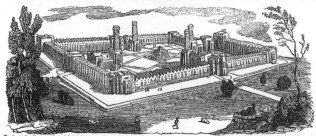

Design of a Community of 2,000 Persons, founded upon a principle, commended by Plato, Lord Bacon, Sir T. More, & R. Owen.

2.13 The impact of scientific thought supplied architects with a further range of associations to support their grandiose claims. These took a number of directions. One derived from Robert Owen's proposition that the behaviour of people could be improved by providing them with appropriate living conditions. His village of Unity and Mutual Cooperation, 'founded upon a principle, commended by Plato, Lord Bacon, Sir T. More, & R. Owen,' was designed by Stedman Whitwell.

2.15 When scientism and global solutions fell into disrepute, architects embraced the arcane realm of metaphysics. This was professionally rewarding at a time when art had come to be merchandised as a luxury consumer product. To its admirers, the Portland Building in Oregon by Michael Graves, completed in 1982, reveals new answers to the meaning of life.

3 Architecture and Culture

Because they follow international styles, architects largely ignore the cultural needs of the communities in which they work.

The idea that buildings should be expressive of the character of the people who live in them is obviously negated by the profession's presumption that architecture is formed by universal (that is, global) ideals or imperatives or interests. The seminal insight of the eighteenth century that a society and its art were (or, more accurately, *ought* to be) related has had only a superficial impact on this situation.

Instead, two different definitions of culture developed side by side to oppose each other. The traditional meaning of culture (akin to 'cultivated') continued to stand for an international élite class of artists and connoisseurs with a belief in absolute standards, and the assumption that it had the requisite learning and taste and talent to recognize and reach them. The new definition of culture came to describe a group of ordinary women and men who lived together in a community and evolved their own institutions, while producing their own artefacts and creating their own values.[1]

Previous Western attitudes had been based on universal systems: of empire or church, or the laws of nature or reason. In contrast, the rise of nationalism, which took place at the turn of the nineteenth century, stressed dissimilarities and uniqueness. The new outlook recognized the existence of definable groups within the human race who expressed themselves through diverse but equally valid means.

The realization that there were various societies with different traits and qualities had existed since merchants and armies began to traverse the world. Europe had already been distinguished from Asia before Alexander the Great marched south and east conquering

Egypt on his way and reaching India.[2] Similarly, ancient writers had marked off northern Europe from the Mediterranean states. The great explorers near the end of the fifteenth century, whose exploits led to the first sea voyage around the globe, completed this process when they made contact with other major human settlements in distant parts of the world.

The response in Europe to this knowledge of other societies was ambivalent.[3] For some, China, or Islam, or the American Indian, represented a utopian ideal. Conversely, many saw non-Europeans merely as savages or heathens to be exploited or converted. Certainly another persistent theme in the history of ideas in Europe has been the assumption of Europe's superiority over the rest of the world and its mission to universalize its own beliefs and values.

This Eurocentric standpoint was undermined by writers in the eighteenth century who attempted to include the various societies of the world in a comprehensive history of the human race. J.G. von Herder, for example, emphasized the diversity of the human population and its organization into a multiplicity of groups with different characteristics.[4] Loosely defining a group as being any community of people with a name and what we now call a culture, Herder studied American Indians and African tribes in much the same way as he studied the Greeks and Romans, thereby setting apart the question whether they were primitive or civilized, and contributing to the conceptual framework that allowed the modern development of anthropology and sociology.

Culture was no longer to be thought of as only an abstract, external, universal ideal but as indigenous to each identifiable group; no longer the exclusive preserve of people of taste, but the natural outcome of social life. This theoretical model was given practical form by the nationalist movements that swept Europe and South America in the wake of Napoleon, who acted both as example and catalyst.[5]

The idea of a national spirit was familiar to architects through Vitruvius who, while discussing the impact of climate on the design of houses, remarked that it also produced the balanced temperament of the Romans, which was the quality that gave them the right to rule the world.[6] Climate (as well as constitution and government) was also used as an explanation when Winckelmann claimed the artistic superiority of the Greeks.[7] Conversely, the influential teacher J.F. Blondel, writing in the *Encyclopédie*, blamed the French climate (and a lack of taste) for the inability of his compatriots to match Classical ornamentation.[8] In turn, the young Goethe's 1773 essay on Strasbourg Cathedral, published by Herder, was entitled 'Of German Architecture,' and passionately rejected French and Italian taste in favour of German genius.[9] A century later, Viollet-le-Duc qualified his appeal to universal reason by contending that 'facts are continually demonstrating that the French brain differs in its construction from that of our neighbours, the English and the Germans,' leading to the conclusion that an architecture relevant to the age must also be in harmony with national conditions and values.[10]

In pressing their cause, the proponents of national sovereignty were able to use this argument and cite architecture, alongside language and religion, as one of the features that distinguished a country's identity. This, reciprocally, strengthened the contention that the style of new buildings should reflect nationalistic sentiment. In Germany, it prompted Friedrich von Schlegel to warn his readers that imitating an alien (Classical) style would only produce an inferior copy while destroying their own indigenous culture.[11] In Britain, it led to the choice of a Neo-Gothic style for the new Houses of Parliament because of its historical associations.[12]

Viewed on its own, without patriotic bias, the logic of this position seemed compelling, a self-evident truth based on ordinary common sense. If climate and materials varied, not to mention a people's way of life, so ought the design of their buildings. Architects of widely different beliefs were therefore motivated to incorporate this axiom into the broader theory (if not the practice) of their work, regardless of their stylistic preferences.

Even the Classicist Soane, who so much admired the French author M.A. Laugier's advocacy of 'original causes' and 'first principles' that he publicly criticized his own work when it failed to reach this standard of perfection, warned his students at the Royal Academy not to think that they could simply copy foreign examples.[13] Certainly they should study Palladio and the other Italian masters, he declared, but too much depended on the local climate, materials, and mode of living for them to be closely imitated.

This discrepancy between theory and practice was to become even more obvious when the Classical tradition was imported into the United States. Actively seeking a new way of life, the American people had made the vision of a New World so much a reality that tens of millions of Europeans emigrated there during the next century. While at first the Classical style (based on the Maison Carrée, Nîmes) was adopted by Thomas Jefferson as a model of beauty and a fitting symbol for the new democratic republic, the call for a more appropriate architectural expression quickly followed. The European-trained immigrant Benjamin Latrobe answered Jefferson that although his principles of taste were also Classical, such precedents had little relevance to American needs. Churches necessarily differed from temples, the country required legislative assemblies rather than basilicas, and the American idea of entertainment was not to be satisfied in amphitheatres.[14] Typically, Latrobe's actual response to the challenge was the Ionic porticoed front of the Bank of Pennsylvania, Philadelphia, and the Soane-like interior of the Catholic Cathedral in Baltimore. His specific design contribution to the symbolic ambitions of the New World was limited to the corn and tobacco plant motifs incorporated into the 'American' Orders used in the United States Capitol.[15]

But if the Classical tradition, with its universal principles and international precedents, allowed little room for the development of an indigenous architecture, the medieval alternative (based on craft rather than aesthetics) seemed to promise a better theoretical base. It was to lead to the first major self-conscious effort to create an architecture that responded more closely to its environmental circumstances.

Again repeating the now common formula that architecture should reflect a country's 'climate, customs, and religion,' Pugin generalized the argument in his attempt to justify the use of the Gothic style in Britain.[16] Insisting that styles were generated by the conditions of their origin, and could not be arbitrarily adopted or imposed, Pugin (though a Catholic convert in a Protestant country) called for a return to medieval practice to recapture the spirit of the British way of life. While his own work (now less known than his detailing of the Houses of Parliament for Charles Barry) closely followed the Gothic style, Pugin stressed the use of local materials and methods, and thereby opened the way to another level of approach. When the full Gothic style, derived from religious buildings, appeared to be insufficiently versatile to satisfy the needs of more recent secular building types, it was superseded as a guide by the vernacular architecture from which it had apparently derived.

For the architects of what became known as the Arts and Crafts movement, the essential principles of good building (leaving aside their embodiment in the Gothic style) were to be discovered in the cottages and barns of the British countryside.[17] At a theoretical level, understanding was to be gained from the way the art of these structures grew out of their social realization, instead of being imposed on them as a style. In practical terms, much was to be learned from their straightforward planning, sensible construction, and general unpretentiousness.

This new recognition of vernacular buildings by those with irreproachable taste like William Morris and Philip Webb marked a major shift in the perception of what constituted aesthetic content. Connoisseurs, architects, and historians had taken centuries to separate architecture from building, art from artefact, labelling one mere craft or product, while extolling the other as an embodiment of metaphysical virtues. The Arts and Crafts advocates argued against this type of division, claiming that vernacular buildings could be aesthetic objects just as rewarding as, or even more than, so-called architecture designed with aesthetic aspirations; and that stemming from the particular needs and means of a given time and place, and infused with the values of the people who made them, such buildings better reflected the society they accommodated.

The design of Red House, Bexley, in 1859 by Webb for Morris, and later houses of the Arts and Crafts movement, sought to return architecture to its vernacular roots.[18] Art was to emerge from the facts of the situation, the enrichment of necessary work, the ordinary made special through good craftsmanship and creative invention. The form of such buildings was seen as a response to the British climate and countryside, to the characteristics of local materials and practices, and to the way of life of their inhabitants.[19]

Equally illustrative of the theoretical implications of vernacular construction, but less publicized and praised, were the more than four hundred schools designed under the direction of E.R. Robson and his successor T.J. Bailey, during the thirty-three-year existence of the London School Board. Contemplating the form to give these schools, Robson abandoned the Gothic style as being too ecclesiastical for the secular instruction required by the 1870 Elementary Education Act. He also rejected what he considered the barrack-like militaristic regimentation of the Prussian model as un-British.[20]

His decision was to follow the lead of his partner, J.J. Stevenson, who had just designed his own house in what became known as the Queen Anne style.[21] Constructed from local yellow stock brick with red brick detailing, the schools erected by the London School Board appeared to grow out of the same order of building as the houses they served, but rose above them physically, psychologically, and socially, their vertical massing enriched by the shaping of their gables and dormers and the accentuation of their pilasters and chimneys.

Unfortunately, none of the more respected architects whose work fell within the orbit of the Arts and Crafts movement had any equivalent success with non-residential buildings. Webb's limited practice and reputation continued to stem from the houses he designed during the forty-one years that followed the initial impact of Red House. In contrast, the personality, imagination, publicity, and prestige of his contemporary, Richard Norman Shaw, undermined the vernacular ideals both men had earlier advocated.[22]

Known for his popularization of the Queen Anne style, Shaw had an exceptional talent that in the end subverted any preoccupation with a theory that would restrict his architectural imagination. New Zealand Chambers in London, completed in 1873, incorporated oriel windows adopted from a seventeenth-century market town house, set between brick piers covering an iron frame, and was capped by an ornamented plastered cove. At New Scotland Yard, built in the following decade, the general form and corner turrets might have been suggested by the name and tradition of the site, an extra ironic twist being the granite base supplied by the convicts from Dartmoor.

Such allusions to other images were a product of a fertile mind, but in neither case could the design be held to follow artlessly from its material conditions and physical context. In these buildings, vernacular motifs such as leaded lights and dormers were as much out of place as the broken pediments or rusticated portals they adjoined. Here, the example of vernacular architecture no longer signified a principled approach to design but had become a style source in itself to be added to the traditional inventory of motifs taken from architectural history – just as it is in much of the Post-Modern style today.

By the new century, even the individuality and character that Shaw had once prized over the imitation of period styles had disappeared and he had reverted to the Classical grand manner with his design for the Baroque colonnade that spanned the front of the upper terrace of London's Piccadilly Hotel. To cite the supplement on 'modern' architecture in the *Encyclopedia Britannica* of the day, British architects had once again embraced some form of Classicism as their professional standard.[23] The return to an unaffected approach to design, eloquently argued by Morris and his disciples, had foundered on the architects' long-standing practice of adopting a style that had no particular relevance to their own time or place.

In the United States, the concurrent attempt to create an indigenous architecture had just come to a similar, but more spectacular, end. As with the forerunners of the Arts and Crafts movement, the initial step by I I.I I. Richardson had drawn its inspiration from medieval Europe. Richardson had trained at the École des Beaux-Arts and worked in Paris during the Second Empire. His choice of southern Romanesque as a working style had important implications, as it marked the first time that an American architect had not followed the current European fashion. Furthermore, he used the style as a visual language rather than as an archaeological model, and was able to imbue his designs with individual qualities that evidently touched the professional mood of the day. Asked in 1885 (the year before he died) to name the ten best buildings in the country, the respondents to an architectural magazine listed five by Richardson, the first by far being Trinity Church in Boston.[24]

Instead of evoking associations with abstract political ideals like 'republican' and 'democratic,' as the earlier imported Graeco-Roman styles had done, his work seemed more particularly to embody and reflect the virtues of the American people – their self-confidence, largeness of conception, and enormous vigour. As with the British experience, the choice of southern Romanesque also led back to the basic art of building. Through his creative enrichment of essential construction, Richardson could make an architectural event out of a downspout or a window frame. In his last great building, the Marshall Field Wholesale Store, the architecture was to be found in the shaping of the outer masonry walls themselves. Here building and architecture merged in the new commercial building types of the period.[25]

If Richardson had found his own way back from the expressive irrelevance of an arbitrarily applied style, other architects were led there by their materialistic clients. The Montauk Block, Chicago, designed by Burnham and Root in the early 1880s, and claimed to be the first office building to be based on a methodical analysis of its requirements, was an early illustration of this process. Asked for a plain brick structure, the architects offered a variety of visual 'improvements' (coloured glass, for example), only to have them turned down as impractical and an unnecessary expense. A few years later the same clients were regretting the eccentricities of the Rookery Building and questioning why Burnham and Root could not follow the admirable example set by Richardson's exteriors.[26]

Other architects with less inventive ability had no difficulty in staying more closely to the utilitarian aspects of design. Practising in an overtly materialistic society with only peripheral concern for aesthetic matters either within or outside the profession, American architects had fewer architectural pretensions than their British counterparts. They did not have to look back to medieval times to re-establish the legitimate origins of their buildings. The tenements, sweatshop lofts, and city warehouses were of the same order as the log cabin: utilitarian structures, once erected for survival and now for the acquisition of wealth.

American architects did not treat these commercial building types as inferior commissions; they could be accepted for what they were – buildings erected for use and profit. The architects' task, therefore, was not so much to strip such buildings of any unsuitable aesthetic dress, as to ennoble them with limited means. This return to elementary considerations of design, which had proved so traumatic for British architects, was for American architects a matter of ordinary practice.

At one level, the Marshall Field Wholesale Store was known for the impressive size of the building and its stone blocks. At another, it was received as a symbol of the American ethos, recorded by Louis Sullivan as a monument to trade and to the power and progress of the age.[27] Its social meaning, as it were, lay in the facts of its site, economics, layout, and daylighting; these, coordinated and integrated, constituted the unadorned building. Later generations were to label such artefacts 'art' and thereby circumvent the issue of how to enhance them with explicit values. For Richardson's younger contemporary Sullivan, however, the challenge was not just to accept the conditions of building as they were, but to shape them so that they celebrated the qualities of being American.[28]

That European nations viewed themselves as different from one another had been demonstrated by more than two thousand years of internecine wars. The worst were still to come; but to those who had left Europe behind, there was a far greater distance between the Old World and the New than between the countries of their ethnic origins. European architects had stressed their dissimilarities of climate, traditions, conventions – even their ways of thought. For Sullivan the distinction was far more profound; at issue was the question of what it meant to be human.

This was to be felt through the writings of a poet like Walt Whitman, whose *Leaves of Grass* was read by Sullivan when he was thirty years old.[29] Whitman's celebration of the spirit of American democracy was an inspiration to Sullivan. Equally so was the stress on individualism and a mystical concordance with nature that closely matched the American experience. Such ideas were to merge in the popular theme that the United States was a favoured nation, the promised land, the home of a chosen people whose manifest destiny was to spread enlightened government across the North American continent.

Here two notions of democracy crossed. The political ideal of liberty was of the sort that encouraged the sporadic attempts of Americans to free Canadians from British rule. Others, including, architects like Sullivan and Wright, viewed democracy in different terms. For these individuals, the collective tradition in religion, government, or art was to be replaced by the human capacity to order one's own world, so that democracy was not a form of government but a society of self-reliant persons, each responsible for, and finding fulfilment in, their own role in life.

For Sullivan, then, the terms old and new, applied to the nations of the Western world, meant those still under authoritarian domination and those free from it. To design in one of the European styles was not just a matter of conservative aesthetics but a mark of spiritual subjection. It followed that the first consequence of being American rather than European was that no imported styles were admissible.

Sullivan simplified the problem of what to use in their place by asserting two propositions. The first was that democracy in the United States had produced the most advanced society in the world and best exemplified the state of civilization in the nineteenth century (a claim also often made by the French). The second was that the tall office building symbolized this new era, in the same way that previous periods had been represented by the temple, cathedral, or palace. Admittedly, the materialistic element in American life might be considered an inhibiting factor, but it could also be a challenge.

This issue was squarely faced by Sullivan in his essay 'The Tall Office Building Artistically Considered.'[30] The British question, 'Can the basis for a valid architecture be found in vernacular building?' was now rephrased to read 'Can vernacular building be turned into valid architecture?' Here, however, 'vernacular' no longer meant traditional materials and crafts but contemporary structural systems and industrialized techniques that provided the common elements for a nation's building needs. His answer was provided in his series of office building designs.

These designs drew their content from two sources. With nature as an analogy, the office building was given its own expressive character through the clarity of its composition, and was thereby ennobled as a building type and imbued with meaning and value as a component of American urban life. In this instance, architecture seemed to emerge from the inherent conditions of the problem itself, instead of being superimposed on it in the guise of a foreign style.

At this stage, Sullivan insisted, the building had only a material existence of its own and still remained, as it were, outside the spiritual realm. Its animation was to come from the ornamentation that enriched his designs. For the building, it enlivened the surface and gave visual immediacy to an otherwise impersonal structure, infusing its form with a sense of organic life. For the architect, it was a manifestation of the democratic ideal, an avowal of his own individuality, and a proof of the power to give shape and existence to inert matter through the act of human creativity.

In subsequent years, the same passionate belief in the uniqueness and specialness of the American experience, the richness of its land, the greatness of its people, and his calling as their prophet, was to be displayed by Frank Lloyd Wright. Here again was the same duality expressed in different terms: the impulse to create a truly American building – the 'prairie' house – as Sullivan had previously hoped to give form and content to the American place of commerce, and the intense individualism that led Wright to denounce those who followed his style instead of his example.[31]

This self-conscious search for an architecture that would express the physical, sociological, and ideological conditions of the New World, was confronted by the Chicago World's Columbian Exposition of 1893. As its centrepiece, huge buildings in Neoclassical forms of simulated marble stood in orderly array around a water basin traversed by gondolas. At the head of this 'court of honor' was the domed and pillared administration building, designed by the doyen of American architects, Richard Morris Hunt, who had been the first of them to study at the École des Beaux-Arts. At the other end, a colossal statue of the 'Republic' by Daniel Chester French (better known for his figure in the Lincoln Memorial) stood in front of a vast peristyle of forty-eight columns, one for each of the states and territories.

Seen by millions of visitors, the fair enthralled commentators with its vision of an ideal city where order and elegance prevailed and one could escape from the ugliness and routine of everyday existence into an enchanted realm of leisure and enjoyment.[32] For some it represented the triumph of (European) civilization over (American) materialism epitomized by Chicago. For many architects, it was conclusive evidence that the Classical tradition was the supreme embodiment of ideal beauty.

In the years leading up to World War I, hundreds of Americans were motivated to go to Paris to study at the École des Beaux-Arts so that they might acquire at its source the knowledge of how to reach this standard of perfection.[33] Conversely, a number of French architects (such as Paul Cret who taught for thirty-four years at the University of Pennsylvania) received appointments at prestigious American universities, where they introduced Beaux-Arts methods of design instruction.[34] Classicism had once again been adopted as the orthodox model of professional taste and its success was to be secured by the example and prestige of the New York firm of McKim, Mead, and White.

McKim had attended the École des Beaux-Arts in the late 1860s. During its early years, his firm had produced a series of resort buildings in a vernacular idiom that corresponded to the approach of the British Arts and Crafts movement. At the same time, however, it also adopted the Italian Renaissance 'palazzo' style for its design of the Villard Houses in New York, and this set the pattern for its major works.

Unlike in Britain, where what was known as the Free Classic style was the prevailing mode of design, the version practised by McKim, Mead, and White was more disciplined.[35] The design for Boston Public Library recalled the Bibliothèque Sainte-Geneviève in Paris and Alberti's Tempio Malatestiano from Rimini. The precedent for New York's Pennsylvania Station, which opened in 1910, was the Roman Baths of Caracalla (with its main room enlarged by twenty per cent). But no matter what the specific detail happened to be, the outcome was the same: the divorce of architecture from its social context, and the reaffirmation of its existence as an idealized art form. The two attempts to create an indigenous architecture in Britain and the United States had been brought to an end by the profession's reversion to its own internal preoccupations.

The Classical form of design that dominated the monumental architecture of the Western world for the next generation ignored issues of time and place because it was conceived as being eternal and universal. There were isolated attempts by individual architects (inspired by the example of a vernacular tradition and the Arts and Crafts philosophy) to create a national architecture in some countries such as Sweden (Ragnar Östberg's Stockholm City Hall) and Holland (Michel de Klerk's housing). There was even an effort to blend the

Classical idiom with non-European features as in Edwin Lutyens' Viceroy's House in New Delhi. But these had little impact on the traditional tendency of the profession internationally to evolve and follow a common style. Moreover, when Neoclassicism fell out of favour among the profession's leaders, it was deposed by another style that was similarly advocated as a universal panacea.

The theory that initially had linked art with society had undermined its own clarity by wavering between nation (community) and time as the locus of a cultural identity. The advocates of the Modern style that replaced Neoclassicism eliminated the problem by assuming that the world was populated by a single human species that had – or ought to have – arrived at the same level of civilization (as defined by some Western Europeans).

Once again, this theoretical stance necessarily ignored any local differences. But this time, its case was given collateral support by the impact of the capitalist system, which tended to eliminate indigenous features as it expanded across the world. Concurrently with industry and commerce, the development of institutions in a worldwide context also brought an increasing unification and imposition of aims and means. Urban plans, offices, industrial plants, mass housing – all felt the impact of their own international networks of specialists, their global production made possible by the technological ability to create the same environment anywhere on earth.

Arguing from this context, the advocates of the Modern style portrayed the image of advanced technology as a primary component of a contemporary architecture. That this was not inevitable had been clearly demonstrated by their predecessors. After all, Sullivan's Guaranty Building had a metal-framed structure and Wright's Unity Temple was constructed out of poured concrete. The underlying issue was whether technology or any other 'state of the art' design component should be viewed as an end in itself, or as another potential tool or instrument through which local social goals might be realized.

Modern architects used technology as a metaphor to reinforce the premise that modern society embraced the whole human race, which, in turn, greatly magnified the scope and importance of the style they were promoting. But in adopting this position, they were part of a general reaction to the excesses of nationalism experienced by many

Western intellectuals. For whereas it had been the populist revolutions of the nineteenth century that had encouraged the idea of
nationalism, it was the two world wars of the twentieth century that
effectively discouraged it.

Germany was the specific example that changed people's minds.
The racial mysticism formulated by a succession of its philosophers,
with their emphasis on the spiritual affinity of the individual and the
state, turned the liberal ideal of nationalism into a conservative doctrine. The estimated ten million dead of World War I underlined
nationalism's inherent dangers. Fear of its consequences was greatly
reinforced by the even more virulent eruption of German racism
under Hitler – paralleled in Japan – that resulted in the slaughter of
countless human beings during World War II.

Such experiences might have convinced anyone of the need for
some form of international cooperation. For many intellectuals, these
lessons were unnecessary. The pursuit of knowledge had always
been international. Architects, too, believed that their designs had
timeless or, at least, universal significance that overrode political or
social divisions, and used the same sort of argument that their
mission was to disclose some absolute truth. This assumption was
formalized and given plausibility by the relatively new discipline of
architectural history.

The architects' perennial claim that their work has great objective
value may easily be attributed to their desire to inflate its importance
for their own advantage. Furthermore, since the Classical tradition
lost its overriding authority as the paradigm of architectural excel-
lence, they have been unable to develop any broadly accepted theory
of general principles on which to base their practice, and the stri-
dency of their assertions seems often to be in inverse proportion to
their credibility. In contrast, architectural historians have created the
appearance of a coherent discipline that observes objective standards.
One result has been that few schools of architecture deal with the
same topics under the subject of 'theory,' whereas most cover the
same buildings in their history courses and assign standard textbooks
that are similar in content.

In reality, however, architectural historians are no more impartial
than the profession they serve. They, too, have an ulterior motive in

supporting the mythology of art, which not only (usually) appeals to
their temperament, but is also the source of their work and livelihood.
In a sense, they constitute the priesthood of art, recording, codifying,
and explaining its mysteries to its devotees. Far from dealing with
objective facts, the subject matter of their study is based on taste.

Out of the millions of buildings that have been erected over the
centuries, the few that are chosen for study are included for a variety
of reasons: that they illustrate the development and spread of a style,
that they seem to have anticipated future events (in hindsight), that
they are great works of art (a property rarely defined), that they are
simply odd and intriguing, or that they were admired by connoisseurs
in their own day or ours. Underlying this selection of subject matter
is a set of theoretical assumptions that are equally questionable.

Three major propositions have rationalized this process. The first
is the architectural specialists' presumption of the objectivity and
infallibility of their own taste, which has caused the study of architectural history to parallel (and add to) the architectural profession's
own arbitrary judgments, and contributed greatly to the partisanship
of the infighting that characterizes architectural politics. The other
two propositions, which reinforce each other, are the notion of the
spirit of the age (or something else very much like it), and its organizing factor, the idea of progress.[36]

By the beginning of the nineteenth century, the notion of the spirit
of the age had been merged with the concept of style as a means of
classifying buildings by their form and character, so that A.L. Millin
in his *Dictionnaire des beaux-arts* was able to divide architectural
works according to their society (Indian, Chinese, Greek, Roman, etc)
or their period (antiquity, middle ages, modern, etc).[37]

This new system was to become an extremely useful tool for architectural historians. It provided a simple explanation why the architecture of different times and places was different. It allowed buildings
of a similar appearance to be grouped together, thereby permitting
them to be compared with and evaluated against each other and a
theoretical model. And, linked with the idea of progress, the system
suggested a chronological pattern of historical development.

The idea of progress had long been familiar in architectural circles.
Alberti had written that the Classical ideal arose in Asia, flowered in

Greece, and reached maturity in Italy.[38] This record was extended by the 'moderns' of the seventeenth century, who believed that their own efforts had added to it. But whereas the idea of progress in social history was normally tied to some significant first or final cause, in architecture it was to become solely a matter of producing a narrative of new styles, each one supplanting the last according to the verdict of the profession's trend-setters.

In consequence, the chronicle of styles that are not controlled by a dominant authority is as inconsistent as the choice of individual buildings within them. Most, like the Classic and Gothic revivals, represented aesthetic positions. Others, such as Italianate, Queen Anne, Secessionist, and one faction of Post-Modernism, have been the cultivated vogue. Still others – rationalists, structuralists – have purported to reveal fundamental truths about the human condition of 'universal man,' regardless of who, where, or when. Similarly, the Modern style took the whole human race as its subject and the planet as its domain. Almost no style has ever been intended to reflect the unique combination of conditions, values, or ambitions of the specific community of people whose buildings it shaped.

Yet by the mid-twentieth century the validity of the assumptions that structure architectural history was largely taken for granted. The main premises of this position were summarized by the eminent art historian Meyer Schapiro in his essay on 'style': that in a given culture or period, there is only one style or a limited range of styles; that these exhibit both significant relationships among themselves, and with other features of their culture; and that a style not only manifests the personality of an artist, but also the broad outlook of a group.[39]

Unfortunately, the harmful consequences of these ideas have been as far-reaching as their academic benefits.[40] The proposition that an architectural style naturally manifests the broad outlook of a group (other than its own supporters) might have seemed justifiable when it was the preserve of a ruling circle that was identified with the state, but made little sense in a new era of democratic societies. The reasoning that had been used to explain the aesthetic products of ancient Greece could not be extended to a world that had passed through the political, technological, economic, social, and demographic revolutions of the eighteenth and nineteenth centuries (when its population had passed the billion mark). This new world was just too complex to lend itself to the simplistic notion that architects intuitively created a 'style or limited range of styles' that reflected the 'broad outlook of a group.'

What they did do was address their own group's interests. This answer might have been deduced from Vico's original statement on the relationship between a society and its institutions. The Italian philosopher had left open the question whether the 'common sense' (his version of 'spirit') of a society was shared by 'an entire class, an entire people, an entire nation, or the entire human race.'[41] Later influential writers were to limit this range of possibilities to the two scales of place and time. But if the locus of styles is taken to be a class, then the production and distribution of styles is readily explicable in terms of the actual mode of practice of architects acting as a distinct group. Architecture does indeed reflect a 'society,' but it is the architects' own professional society that it reflects.

Looking back, it is evident that the production and distribution of styles has been essentially an internal process. Long ago, architecture might have symbolized the beliefs, values, or concerns of its community as a whole, but it has not done so for many centuries. Certainly, styles nowadays must be acceptable to the architects' employers. But where architects are left to control their own styles, any correspondence between them and the public realm is largely fortuitous.

In reality, each social situation offers countless circumstances, ideas, and images that may be drawn upon to shape the design of buildings. Architects choose those that support their designs. To imply, as architectural historians do, that (talented) architects alone respond to the only valid influences of their time or place, simply takes the architects' own estimation of their work at its face value and tries to find justifications for it.

For example, proponents of the Modern style were fascinated by automobiles, ocean liners, and airplanes. They could have been inspired by huts and tents. They turned to logic to solve their problems. They could have used the advice of other specialists. They cited Marx and Einstein. They could have drawn on the writings of Émile Durkheim or Franz Boas. Alternatively, they might have relied on tradition, incremental change, and common sense.

Additionally, influences are not limited to the events of a particular period. The past is also a repository of sources. That is why Post-Modern architects may use Palladian windows or developers' housing may carry mansard roofs. Even architects of the Modern style, who prided themselves on being up to date, might be said – at least from an English-speaking standpoint – to have combined their contemporary belief in the efficacy of science and technology with a nineteenth-century code of morality and an eighteenth-century sense of taste. In this process, styles do not result from non-architectural circumstances; they receive their motivations and justifications from them. The test of their success is not whether they reflect the spirit of the age but whether they satisfy the interests of their public.

As with production, so with distribution. The introduction of the Modern style into other countries had no bearing on its relationship with the 'machine age' that was supposed to be its generative cause. On the contrary, when it arrived in Britain, 150 years after the Industrial Revolution began, it was through the activities of immigrants from the (underdeveloped) colonies (especially the New Zealander Amyas Connell) and a Russian émigré (Lubetkin).[42] Similarly, it was taken to the United States, another established industrial power, by the Austrians Rudolph Schindler and Neutra, and the Swiss William Lescaze. In both cases, the dissemination of the new style took place through the profession itself and had little to do with the local population.

This procedure is nothing new. When the Renaissance style was introduced into other European countries, it too took place through the same sort of network, although then its sponsors were the nobility. In France, the new style was imported by feudal lords and the royal court, which later invited Italians such as Sebastiano Serlio to demonstrate its merits.[43] A century later, when Inigo Jones carried back its Palladian principles and forms from his Italian tour, they were first displayed in the buildings he designed for the queen and as Surveyor of the King's Works.[44]

In their practice, architects have followed their own self-interest; that is why it is possible to discuss architecture in its own autonomous terms. Because styles are generated by architects rather than circumstances, each tends to follow the last in a biblical-like sequence of procreation. Architects generally imitate their leaders as if that were the incontestable thing to do (probably as a result of the illusion that they personify universal or timeless truths). Consequently, styles are copied everywhere without regard for any local compatibility and take on an international appearance.

It is this process that architectural historians have rationalized and legitimated. The result is that architectural history is often presented as a single narrative of styles moving from one centre of (collective or individual) genius to another – Greece, Rome, France, Italy ... Victor Horta, Le Corbusier, Robert Venturi – each responsible for contributing the significant architecture of its (or his) time. To achieve this appearance of a logical sequence, the system has to exclude all discordant elements.

One major omission must be the architecture of non-Western countries that do not fit the general thesis. Another equally important if less obvious distortion stems from the differences among Western nations themselves. These are basically ignored by the architectural historian's paramount need to produce a continuous narrative of a global march of events. Under these conditions, no story concerning the architecture of any country is ever completed. The 'Greek' story is limited to Classical Greece; the 'Italian' story to ancient Rome and the Renaissance and Baroque (and possibly Neo-Rationalism); the 'British' story to assimilated imports, stylistic revivals, and the Arts and Crafts movement; the 'American' story to the Chicago School and late- and Post-Modernism. As for the architecture of large areas of the Western world such as the Iberian peninsular, Scandinavia, the Balkan states, even Russia, let alone ex-colonies like Canada or Australia, such countries are not even credited with an architecture worth consideration except for the designs of an occasional talented individual. The result has been to treat tens of millions of people as if they lacked their own culture, and to devalue and undercut any attempt by architects to contribute to it.

In short, architectural historians have minimal interest in relating architecture, that is building, to its social context, but simply mirror the profession's mythic view of itself. A style's adoption by the profession is accepted as proof of its significance. Its spread among the profession is taken to show it has universal validity. The rejection of an existing style by the profession is treated as an indication of its obsolescence. The endorsement of a new style by the profession is interpreted as a sign of progress.

Even more, influential architectural historians have actively engaged in promoting the architects' view that their work has a transcendental value that overrides local considerations. For example, while (supposedly impartially) recording and explaining the Modern style, Nikolaus Pevsner carefully picked 'pioneers' from an assortment of countries to illustrate how the ultimate expression of the spirit of the twentieth century was finally synthesized by Walter Gropius.[45] Sigfried Giedion invoked Einstein to show that Modern art and architecture were the inevitable response to a new (twentieth-century) cosmic sense of space.[46] More down-to-earth but just as partisan, Hitchcock and Johnson labelled Modern architecture 'international,' when there were only a few examples of it to be found anywhere in the world.[47]

This, of course, is what the architects of the Modern style wanted it to be seen as: an updated replacement for the Neoclassical style – which was still, in fact, the 'international' style of the profession. In this contest, it was also to be portrayed as being above nationality – that is, universal if not eternal – the only authentic style for the new global society. Yet regardless of the long-standing preference of the architectural world to deal in idealized styles outside the public realm (and any control it might exert), the social dilemma for the individual remained, caught between the magnitude and complexity of the world at large and the urge to belong to some recognizable part of it.

The problem was to be poignantly illustrated by Sibyl Moholy-Nagy in her biography of her husband, who once taught at the Bauhaus, the school of design that superseded the École des Beaux-Arts as the symbolic centre of the international profession. In his thirties, imbued with the belief that art was international, László Moholy-Nagy is described rejecting contemptuously the arguments of the Russian film director, Sergei Eisenstein, who refused to leave the U.S.S.R. because a 'man can't live without a country.' Ten years later, an immigrant in Chicago, Moholy-Nagy is seen founding the Council for a Democratic Hungary and, subsequently, uttering his dying words in Hungarian.[48]

In the wider world, the same contradictions had occurred. Liberal intellectuals might have denounced nationalism as an agent of human conflict, but groups without countries of their own used it as a rallying cry in their struggle for independence. Rather than containing this demand, the impact of the two world wars encouraged it. The drive for self-determination had been gathering momentum since the American Revolution. During the following century, various groups achieved their separate existence as nations. The most celebrated occasion was the Greek liberation from Turkish rule; the most extensive was the emancipation of the Latin American states from Spain and Portugal. This trend continued unabated before and after World War I. Finland, Poland, and the Baltic states separated from Russia, Albania from Turkey, Norway from Sweden, Ireland from Britain.

With the United Nations' adoption of the principle of self-determination as a key element of its charter, the process reached its peak after World War II, when large areas of Asia and Africa were freed from colonial rule.[49] It erupted again with the breakup of the Communist bloc. Consequently, during the same period that the notion of the world as a 'global village' became commonplace, when multinationals and the media traversed the globe, and Europe and other regions moved towards greater economic and political cooperation, the number of independent states in the world more than doubled.[50] These states ranged in population from the more than a billion inhabitants of China to the few thousand who lived in Nauru. Seemingly, while certain human needs and activities were to be realized at an international scale, others were to be fulfilled at a local level.

Given the new awareness of non-Western societies, the nature of their relationship to an international architectural style was to have a major impact on the theory of its advocates. This took place in different phases. Following the tradition in the West of taking for granted its superiority over other races – and ignoring the fact that the Western nations contained less than one-third of the world's population – its architects had long assumed that their art best represented human civilization as a whole. The liberation movements in Asia, Africa, and the Middle East did nothing to substantially alter this view. Neither, initially, did the realization that coun-

tries like China or India or Iran had equally important heritages of
their own.

Interaction between the architecture of the West and other civiliza-
tions had taken visible form with the Chinoiserie vogue of the eighteenth century, which was merged with the Rococo and Neo-Gothic
modes of design.[51] Conversely, once Europeans had conquered other
territories such as the Indian subcontinent, they took with them their
own architectural conventions and motifs, which they used in the
buildings they erected in their colonies.[52] To the extent that styles
were intermingled regardless of their source, it could be argued that
this process had been a normal outcome of social intercourse on an
international scale. It could also be perceived in fundamentally different terms by the groups involved. While Europeans felt free to adopt
whatever they liked from other cultures, for colonized countries,
Neoclassical or other Western images could be read as symbols of
political, economic, or military repression, clearly alien to the countries where they were implanted. Their use stemmed more from the
design norms of whatever parent institutions they represented – the
imperial government, one of the Christian churches, commercial
enterprises – than from any consideration of the cultural values of
the local society.

With the increasing independence of non-European states and the
spread of the Modern style, the nature of the symbolic connection
between the two altered dramatically. Instead of being seen as a sign
of colonial subservience, the importation of Modern architecture came
to be equated with prestige and progress. This change of attitude
followed naturally when, freed from colonial rule, the new nations
themselves looked to the West for technical assistance.

In the field of architecture, Western architects set up educational
programs with the same subjects and methods (and sometimes exactly the same design problems) as those of Western schools.[53] Other
students were sent abroad by their governments to receive their
architectural training in the international style. Foreign architects
were encouraged to establish offices in their host countries or provided their services from afar. There was little thought that the
intrinsic nature of the design taught or offered by Western architects
held any problems for the local population.

By this time the forms of Modern architecture were taken for granted and the style largely conceived in functional terms. At most, then, it was thought that the style would only have to be modified to take into account local conditions such as climate, customs (which might affect the arrangement of the plan), and available materials and techniques. In a functionalist rationale, the incorporation of this specialized knowledge was no different in kind from the general process of design applied to any ordinary project. Furthermore, architects trained to think in terms of universal principles and international styles saw buildings in other countries merely as regional variants of their own normal practice. The fact that design carries with it intrinsic specific cultural values was realized neither by the non-Western nations nor by those whose help they solicited and received.

Of course there were exceptions. In his pre–World War II essay 'In Praise of Shadows,' the notable Japanese author Tanizaki Jun'ichiro eloquently regretted that Western inventions had altered the traditional Japanese mode of living; that the replacement of lacquered wood seats by white porcelain toilets had turned a ritual into a function, and that the alien presence of the electric stove had brought to an end the pleasure of family gatherings around the glowing coals of the hibachi. Even the Western treatment of such seemingly 'abstract' architectural elements as light had made a substantial impact on Japanese notions of beauty.[54] For whereas Western architects might assume that such architectural qualities were culturally neutral in their design, resulting from the objective demands of architecture itself, they could also be seen by others as distinctly Western in origin, the sort of thing a 'Western' mind would conceive in response to its own situation.

This was definitely a minority view. More typically, after World War II, the leaders of non-Western countries actively embraced Western images as proof of their political, social, economic, or industrial maturity. The Modern style sprang up in Lagos, Jidda, Singapore. The most famous of these incursions took place at Chandigarh, where Le Corbusier was requested by its British-educated prime minister, Jawaharlal Nehru, to create a city that would be a symbol of the new India unfettered by the (unwholesome) traditions of its past.[55]

Commissioned in 1950, the design of Chandigarh might have provided the ultimate proof for the profession that it had created a universal architecture for the modern age. Unfortunately, the new generation of avant-garde architects was in the process of shifting its ideological ground and thereby undercutting the achievements of its heroes. This change in position was signalled at the 1959 meeting of CIAM which, thirty-one years before, had proclaimed the birth of the movement.

Pressed by the Japanese Kenzo Tange to show how his design for a new town differed from the utopian prescriptions of Le Corbusier (then, at age seventy-one, CIAM's elder statesman), the Dutchman Jacob Bakema was defended by the Italian Giancarlo de Carlo. Le Corbusier's proposals, he contended, had been in the form of a general response to the problems of architecture and urbanism, whereas Bakema's plans were based on the specific needs of postwar Holland.[56] If it would be difficult to show how Bakema's mixture of de Stijl (abstract, universal art) and Corbusian (doctrinaire) elements was specifically Dutch in the national meaning of the term, de Carlo was more revealing in his own work and his justification of it.[57]

De Carlo, then thirty-nine years old, accepted the orthodox belief that Le Corbusier was a genius but admonished him for mistaking the metaphysical or 'phantascientific' for 'life,' and called for the reawakening of a 'historical consciousness.' Even more unusual in the context of the Modern style was de Carlo's proposition that architecture should be guided along new 'national tracks,' where it could become part of the living fabric of the communities it served.

This proved to be too heretical for de Carlo's avant-garde colleagues, despite their manifestos. Both his own work in southern Italy with its arcades and pitched roofs, and the firm of BBPR's more widely known Torre Velasca office/apartment block in Milan with its silhouette reminiscent of a medieval tower, were criticized by other members of the group, who disdained such seemingly conservative and superficial devices. If the Modern credo was to be replaced, it had to be by another cause that was equally all-embracing. This was supplied by Aldo van Eyck, who gave the meeting an alternative abstract vision of the relationship between society and architecture.

As with Kahn, who paralleled and overshadowed him in the years ahead, van Eyck's importance arose from the great significance that he attached to the practice of architecture, and the poetic metaphors through which this was described. Van Eyck, like de Carlo, argued that the Modern movement had overstressed its break with the past, but he proposed a different response. In opposition to the idea of a machine age society of faceless masses, he posited a sentient human being, seeking fulfilment in existence. People were always essentially the same; the architect's role was to assist their 'homecoming.'[58]

Tradition, history, or culture were not to be found in images grafted onto buildings, but in the varying reactions of individuals with different backgrounds to architectural situations responding to innate human, spiritual needs. In another architectural aphorism, this was summed up as: 'Whatever space and time [the old Modern style keywords] mean, place and occasion mean more.' This ideal of 'place-making,' a term endorsed by Kahn, was to dominate architectural thinking over the succeeding decades.[59]

The widespread appeal of the new mythology was due to a number of considerations. It proclaimed that the same universal principles were to be found embedded in the buildings of all ages, and especially in those of primitive societies (for example, the Dogon, visited by van Eyck), thereby accentuating the idea of fundamental human characteristics and behaviour that transcended time and locality. It also allowed for a new fusion of universal and historical positions by treating any admired design element as a manifestation of a general rule (although, of course, the connection would be presented by its advocates in the opposite sequence). It therefore permitted a broader scope than Kahn's concurrent emphasis on archetypal solutions, while similarly ennobling the architect's role by attributing to it a profound depth of meaning. This move was in turn reinforced by its connection to other current interests such as structuralism.

Perhaps most of all, the popularity of the notion of 'a sense of place' lay in its accessibility to the ordinary members of the profession who had been brought up in the Modern manner. In practical terms, its advocacy left the Modern style intact. Possibly, instead of arranging a plan within a given aesthetic of space and form relationships, architects might emphasize parts of their buildings as elements delineating certain social rituals. But this had little impact on the general characteristics of their designs. The attitude to materials and structure, to claims of honesty and rationality, to geometry and light, to form and space as abstract qualities, to architecture as a universal system – these remained unchanged. For the majority of architects, only the rhetoric had altered.

This innovation was to have considerable importance in the decades ahead. In the massive verbal assault on the Modern style that occurred from the late 1960s onwards, the accusation that its advocates had tried to wipe the slate clean and invent a universal utopia found a ready audience among those captivated by the alternative mystical notion of 'place.'

Now architects themselves denounced the Modern style and the internationalism they had previously demanded. Instead of celebrating Le Corbusier's design for Chandigarh as the culmination of the contribution of a generation of architects, critics condemned it, alleging that it ignored traditional living patterns.[60] Roads planned for automobile traffic were said to carve sun-drenched ribbons of paving through the city. The familiar bazaars had been replaced by isolated rows of shops. Women, accustomed to preparing food on the floor, were forced to use European-styled kitchens. It was argued that although Le Corbusier might have thought he was bringing Indian society into line with twentieth-century life, he had largely ignored the indigenous culture of Chandigarh's inhabitants.

Once this issue concerning the likely conflict between Western-style architecture and non-Western conditions was recognized, the same argument could be made regarding Western nations outside the style-making centres. In Canada, for example, the Modern movement's fixation with glass (and its associated significations) was noticeably out of place in a land of climatic extremes. Even more important, however, if less obvious, was the misfit between the underlying assumptions of the imported style and local traditions and values. As a pluralistic society, the inhabitants of Canada have always had a need to create or defend their own sense of identity, especially to distinguish Canada from the United States, Quebec from the rest of Canada, and native groups from everyone else. In adopting the Modern style, Canadian architects largely obliterated ethnic as well as regional differences, and turned Canadian cities into replicas of their American counterparts. Far from being the answer to all architectural problems, the Modern style could be seen as a form of cultural imperialism, carried out by an easily deluded profession with little understanding of its social responsibilities.

Le Corbusier's 'society' had been the abstract accompaniment of economics and politics, an anonymous faceless mass, organized and cared for by its leaders – among whom architects claimed a place. Van Eyck attempted to humanize this mass, but still conceived individuals in generalized terms with universal, behaviourist characteristics. These in turn were presented in an idealized way, so that the architect's world was inhabited by feeling, sensitive, receptive people – in a word, perfect human beings. Given the actualities of the real world, it was left to the Americans to depict an ordinary contemporary society and people as they were with all their inconsistencies and flaws.

Here the issue was directly posed. Historically, architectural styles had been portrayed as emanating from the most progressive elements of civilization. Styles were imported not because they best suited the community that acquired them, but because they were received as the most advanced state of their art by the profession. Such styles were usually viewed as being essentially outside questions of nationality. Modern architecture was expected to be equally at home to French art lovers, the Soviet proletariat, or the British upper middle class. The Dutch Structuralism propagated by van Eyck was assumed to be meaningful to any wholesome, sensitive human being. The Italian Neo-Rationalism of Aldo Rossi appealed to the collective memory of the human race, or at least the civilized part of it. Within this framework of ideas, the concept of regionalism was reserved for minor modifications of the preferred style due to local requirements, or as a sort of folk art in marginal countries on the periphery of global events.

The United States filled neither condition of being marginal or provincial. The days had long passed since Charles Dickens' fledgling architect Martin Chuzzlewit had been overwhelmed by its crude materialism. It had become the world's foremost superpower, and New York had replaced Paris as the art centre of the Western world. Instead of being merely the recipient of European styles, supplemented by the work of a few native-born talents, the United States had become the originating source, for the artists of other nations to denounce, envy, and imitate. The quintessential Western man of the architect's imagination was not to be found in the European capitals, but in New York and California, where the latest styles flourished and received acclaim and financial reward. Now the Europeans were the provincials, taking their fantasies and images from that promised land across the sea, surrogate purveyors of an alien culture. Even when pop art originated in London before it was developed in the United States, its ingredients were American – Hollywood sex, Detroit styling, Madison Avenue advertising.[61]

The problem was that this society could not be conceived in abstract idealized terms. To a large degree, the American stereotype had retained the discreditable features of its vulgar forefathers. Unlike the European model human being, its American counterpart was a person of flesh and blood, sometimes in a grey suit, sometimes in a flowered shirt, enterprising, brash, both beneficiary and victim of the most advanced capitalist society in the world. But it was this society, this sense of place, this context, that a new set of American architects were intent on celebrating.

Introduced by Robert Venturi in a house constructed for his mother in 1963, the new Post-Modern style reflected a number of specifically American conditions and concerns. Modern architects had attempted to create new universal building types out of abstract geometric forms. Later architects had sought their ideal form in some more anthropological primordial past. Venturi (and his partners) argued that greater meaning and relevance could be achieved through designs that exploited the qualities of ordinary building types that had evolved from everyday life. In focusing on the American scene, he accepted the 'ugly and ordinary' as an inevitable and vital component of American society.[62] Important architectural lessons were to be learned from the highway strip, the roadside drive-in, the suburban home, advertising signs.

By posing the question 'is not Main Street almost all right?', Venturi illuminated many aspects of the theoretical basis of architecture.[63] For more than a century through the Arts and Crafts Exhibition Society, the Wiener Werkstätte, the Deutscher Werkbund, the

Bauhaus, and numerous other 'make the world beautiful' groups, Europeans had been trying to 'raise' the public appreciation of 'good' design with a conspicuous lack of success – much to their surprise.

Venturi looked back unashamedly on a different tradition – the land of Sinclair Lewis' Babbitt and the commercial impulse that had fashioned it. Immersed in their visions of some utopia, architects would like to impose their sense of order on the world, but Americans had never lived that way and there was little evidence that they wished to do so. The promised land was far messier, more open, crass, vital, human, like its inhabitants. The buildings they had erected for themselves were not to be disdainfully dismissed but represented the up-to-date sum of their collective endeavours over the past few centuries. Gridiron lots, standard plans, common materials, stock building components, normal practices – this was the 'vernacular' on which to base an American architecture, just as architecture had been made out of the commercial office block.

The lesson restated yet again was that good taste was a learned convention, and that artefacts could be as eloquent as artworks in their expression of a culture. Obviously, much of the art-world fame that accrued to Venturi derived from his unusual (for the time) knowledge of architectural history and his use of it in an avant-garde manner. He and his partners could also cite semiology in their investigation of highway signs, which led to their proposition that architecture could be conceptualized as a decorated shed. Whatever the reasons for the reputation of the Venturi partnership, it focused attention on the distance between the symbol systems of the general public and the profession, and the differences in their means of communication.

In terms of European history, this suggested a way of closing the rift that had occurred with industrialization and the rise of the specialized designer. Within the American context, it was a timely reminder that the United States was a freewheeling nation that expected its tastes to be indulged, not enforced. Europeans had been brought up to look to their 'betters' as the objective authority on aesthetic standards, even when they could not understand or appreciate them. Americans were more used to voicing their own prejudices and seeking their own more worldly gratification.

It was these expectations that Venturi's contemporary, Charles Moore, addressed.[64] Where Venturi dealt with the physical reality of his country, Moore explored the psyche of its people. Appropriating the idea of the creation of 'place' as the architect's responsibility, Moore stripped it of its metaphysical pretensions. In various partnerships, he set out purposefully to design environments that would provide an appropriate setting for the activities of their inhabitants – in other words, to create as an architect the sort of symbolic content that primitive groups had once instinctively incorporated into the making of their artefacts. Whereas the functionalist bias of the Modern style had earlier stressed the materialistic determinants of this activity, Moore advocated their reintegration into a broader sociocultural purpose. Rationality and utility were only one side of the human condition. To these must be added reverie and fantasy if the human spirit was to be engaged.

To achieve this end, images could be drawn from diverse sources, collated and integrated, to form a collage of references, allusions, associations, juxtapositions that engrossed the memory and the mind. Motifs and ideas culled from vernacular traditions, everyday practices, and architectural history, were layered both figuratively and literally in Moore's own original stylistic manner. If the result had overtones of Hollywood, a film set on which to play out the drama (or comedy) of existence, then that was at one with the American genius, to have aggressively sought a new way of life and to have created the necessary myths to sustain it. Here was an architecture in the service of real people, not 'society,' not 'man,' but ordinary people. The question was, was it really architecture?

Architecture, unlike building, had always been thought of as profound because it did not deal with ordinary human beings – at least, not unless they were conceived in heroic or abstract or ideal terms (that is, if they were considered at all). In accepting and responding to the American way of life, Venturi and Moore had adapted their forms to a culture that was widely known to have serious imperfections. Yet this did not prevent them from gaining international renown. Their originality, talent, erudition, and status – Moore had headed two prestigious schools of architecture – assured their place as art-world heroes. So did their subject matter – the American scene

– which repelled and attracted, but always fascinated, people around the world.

In the circumstances, their example could have led to a better understanding of the purpose of architecture. But given the traditional attitudes of the profession, it had a different impact. Far from being received as a reasoned basis on which to construct an architecture derived from social considerations, their work was seen mainly as a release from the constraints of the Modern style, and encouragement for the free expression of the artistic imagination. Here architecture again embraced the 'art for art's sake' doctrine, ignoring the people for whom it was built, and reasserting its role as a product for the international art set. Yet another attempt to create an architecture for the people who used it was to be subverted by the profession, which went on to explain the change in style as the inevitable consequence of what was dubbed a decentred era.

None the less, the American initiative by Venturi and Moore held considerable significance for communities everywhere. Architectural critics often dismissed designs of local or regional value as 'provincial,' meaning mediocre, this being one of their arsenal of derogatory terms used to disparage those who might challenge their established positions concerning 'art.' The example of Venturi and Moore undermined this argument. By making ordinary people and their buildings the measure and motivation of design rather than some abstract, universal, or fictional ideal, they had opened the way for each community – however that might be defined – to explore its own values in architectural terms. The subject matter of architecture had been dislodged from its transcendental plane and brought back into the public realm. The problem now was how to convince the profession that architecture could arise from such commonplace roots.

3.1 The notion of culture that developed in the nineteenth century acknowledged that the human race had evolved into many different groups, each with its own language, institutions, beliefs ... and architecture. An Inuit igloo.

3.2 Architects had great difficulty with the idea that buildings should reflect the conditions and values of their own communities. They knew it made good sense, but could not fit it into their preconceptions. Accustomed to using the international styles of their day, they could only bring themselves to add a few local touches like the 'corn-cob' columns Benjamin Latrobe devised for the United States Capitol in 1809.

3.3 A renewed interest in local materials and methods of construction led some architects to try to design buildings that would fit into their surroundings. A London School Board school of 1886 by its architect, E.R. Robson, alongside terraces of brick houses.

3.4 Other architects looked back to their country's heritage to find the elements of an indigenous style. Stockholm City Hall (1909–23) by Ragnar Östberg.

3.5 A few architects, like Michel de Klerk and Piet Kramer, relied on their own inventiveness to express the character of their communities. These apartments in Amsterdam were built in the 1920s.

3.6 Isolated attempts to create buildings that reflected social conditions and values were eclipsed by the continued use of the Neoclassical style in vast civic projects such as the National Gallery of Art in Washington. It was designed by John Russell Pope in 1937, the same year that Albert Speer produced his monumental master plan for Hitler's Berlin.

3.7 After World War II, the Neoclassical style was replaced by its updated version, the Modern style. A postwar housing estate in London.

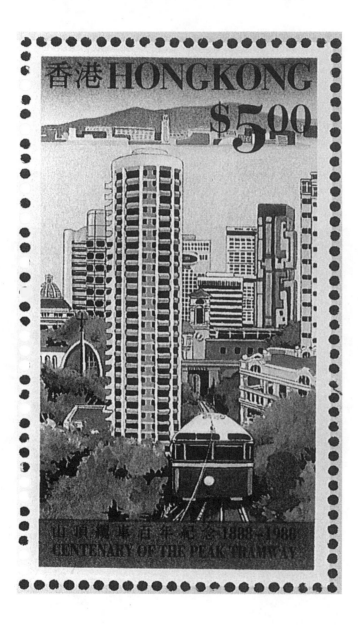

3.8 Seen as a symbol of progress, the Modern style swept the world without regard for history or geography. A Hong Kong stamp commemorates a century of technological development.

3.9 New possibilities were opened up in the 1960s and 1970s with the debunking of the current architectural dogma by Robert Venturi and his colleagues Denise Scott Brown and Steven Izenour. But architects once again went their own way.

3.10 In Mississauga City Hall, for example, which opened in 1987, Edward Jones and Michael Kirkland attempted to combine forms from local Ontario building types with the 'Nordic Classicism' that was used in Sweden sixty years earlier. The question remains: How can the architectural needs of a community be met when architects indulge their own particular tastes?

4 Culture and Class

*Architects think they have the right
to impose their own tastes on everyone else.*

Because they believe that their designs owe a higher allegiance to an
abstract ideal, architects have been unable to respond to the needs of
their own communities. The same assumption has also enabled them
to dismiss out of hand the aesthetic values of the majority of their
fellow citizens. When architects worked directly for the powerful and
the rich, it was natural for them to assume that the tastes they shared
were better than those of the common people they dominated. The
widespread success of capitalism stripped architects of their influential support and left them to defend their superiority on the basis of
their special expertise. Caught in this predicament, they bolstered
themselves by condemning others who threatened their position.
Their main target was the newly expanded middle class, to which,
paradoxically, architects were ultimately to belong. The two centuries
following the Industrial Revolution were marked by the profession's
attempts to maintain its privileged standing against the increasing
impact of this traditional scapegoat.

The belief that some societies could be considered more artistic
than others flourished during the Renaissance when ancient Rome
was rediscovered as the fashionable ideal. According to Alberti, the
Romans had been so discriminating that even their drains were
beautiful.[1] This reverence for a bygone culture was soon transferred
to contemporary Florence itself, where Italians first reaffirmed their
Classical heritage. It was this idea that humankind had entered upon
another golden age that ultimately allowed Palladio to feel sufficient
pride in his own designs to publish them alongside drawings of

antique buildings as if they were their equal.[2] Classical Rome and Renaissance Italy had come to be thought of as the two societies in the existence of the Western world where civilization had peaked.

This view persisted until the second half of the eighteenth century when, with the rediscovery by Western Europeans of Greece, which had been under Turkish rule for three hundred years, Athens replaced Rome as the Classical ideal. Given the new sense of history, the question could now be asked why such nations excelled in the arts. As we have seen, Winckelmann's answer with respect to Greece was to argue that its arts had flourished because they were nurtured by its physical and social environment.[3] Once this premise that superior societies produced superior art was accepted, it was a short step to argue that the converse was also true.

For Chambers, who championed the Roman cause, Greece could not have created outstanding works of architecture because it was just a small country divided into many states with few resources and inadequate means.[4] In this line of reasoning, buildings were a reflection or symbol of a society's worth. Inferior societies must necessarily produce inferior art. The nineteenth century was soon to be denounced as the most extreme example of this proposition.

Whatever primary source it looked back upon, the Classical tradition supported the idea that architecture embodied profound aesthetic qualities. Equally impressive, the Gothic tradition seemed to reflect the spiritual essence of life. The Middle Ages, latecomer to the select company of Athens, Rome, and Florence, had been elevated to this position by the ideas and literature of the late eighteenth century onwards. Its new reputation was soon assimilated into the mainstream of architectural thought where, enthusing over the ingenuity, awesomeness, and spirituality of the quintessential Gothic cathedral, writers declared it to be the equal of the recently glorified Greek temple.

Sharply contrasting with these salutary qualities of the age of faith and the age of antiquity, the age of capitalism seemed to its critics to cast a long shadow over society and the arts. Its agents were deemed to belong to the new middle class, which sought its income from banking, commerce, and industry, or from financial speculation, and whose dominating interest was the accumulation of wealth. Previously few in number with limited status and power, this expanded middle class acquired both as economic and political events in Britain and France during the early nineteenth century favoured its success.

The old middle class of professionals and businessmen had known its place in the earlier social order. The *nouveaux riches* quickly left behind their frugal ways and sought to imitate the behaviour of their social superiors, or ostentatiously indulged their own preferences. In either case, the result seemed to their belittlers a travesty of all that was considered to be the correct expression of breeding, wealth, and taste. The bourgeois wore the wrong clothes, chose the wrong furniture, admired the wrong art. Worse still, if he was a factory owner and British, he destroyed the beauty of the countryside and filled the world with ugliness through the mass production of goods marked by shoddy materials, poor workmanship, and tawdry effects.

Given this view of the situation, the critics of nineteenth-century taste reacted in three substantially different ways. The aesthetes in the 'art for art's sake' movement renounced all connection between society and the arts and denied that the public taste was any of their concern. The more radical aesthetes argued that art and society were organically linked, and insisted that nothing could be done to raise the standard of public taste until society itself had been fundamentally restructured. Conventional aesthetes proposed to remedy the problem through public education.

As it turned out, all three groups had a lasting impact on the issue. The force and persuasiveness of the radical critics carried the day in terms of their theoretical analysis of the situation. The practical proposition that the public could be taught to appreciate the specialist's taste was embedded in the educational system. And the subsequent accomplishments of all three groups confirmed the 'art for art's sake' assertion that there was no intrinsic or necessary relationship between what had become known as 'art' and people (or society) at large.

These three positions overlapped and often merged. The 'art for art's sake' movement took its popular form from French literary and artistic circles, where it coincided with the victory of middle class interests under Louis Philippe. Especially for the aristocracy, making fun of bourgeois manners had been a long-standing tradition in

France; Molière's *Le Bourgeois Gentilhomme* was first performed for Louis XIV at the royal château at Chambord. By transferring their antipathy towards prevailing artistic conventions to the unwitting middle class, the creative personalities of the nineteenth century, nettled by their own critics, found a ready-made enemy on which to transfer their frustrations.

If critics were narrow-minded, moralistic, and reactionary, they were merely espousing bourgeois values to advance their popularity and their sales.[5] They were only the symptom, not the cause. The real enemy was the middle class. In the aesthete's lexicon, a bourgeois was anyone who had no true understanding of the arts. That certainly seemed to include the bourgeois stereotype. Materialistic and untutored, the grasping, mean-spirited man (and woman) of affairs came to stand for everything that was antagonistic to genuine artistic creativity.

Rejecting this philistine society obsessed with making money, a new generation of artists declared itself with flowing hair and colourful clothes. The outcome of this rejection of the Classical tradition was the fanciful land of Bohemia, where youthful talent might be forced to suffer poverty in a garret, yet still find happiness in comradeship and love while waiting for recognition and acclaim. There, artists withdrew into their own company, severing the ties between art and the outside world. Casting the century adrift, or dissecting it from the sidelines, its adversaries felt free to condemn its unsavouriness while protecting the incorruptibility of their own reputations.

In practice, nineteenth-century events proved that the despised materialistic qualities of the age had little discernible effect on the production of the art world. From Hugo to Verlaine, from Turner to Whistler, through Wagner and Brahms, the inexorable rise of capitalism did nothing to stem the flow of what the art world terms creative genius. If something was lacking, it was not creative talent but public recognition of it.

Of course the question was whether the artists of the time were even attempting to satisfy the symbolic needs of society at large or simply gratifying their own or, as they would say, obeying the demands of 'art' itself. Furthermore, the basic assumptions that the profit motive underlying mass production was necessarily antagonistic to art, and that art was too refined for ordinary people to appreciate, were disproved by the success of a writer like Dickens, whose monthly instalments attracted numerous readers from all social classes.[6] Such doubts were swept aside by the critics who had determined that bourgeois taste was bad, and that this was the issue to be faced and resolved.

The claim that art was autonomous, that is, outside the social realm, sustained the idea that humankind could be divided into those who understood art, and those who did not. It separated the informed élite from the uninitiated; the creative artist from the common mob. For poets and painters, this division might have held little material consequence. The former probably expected to have a limited appeal; the latter needed only a very few wealthy admirers. For what might be called loosely 'designers,' the situation was essentially different.

Like novelists who had to establish a large reading audience if they wanted to live on the proceeds from their writing, product designers had to please the buying public. In a similar if not identical way, architects had to please their clients. No longer mainly from the aristocracy, which had once shared and even shaped the architect's interests, these clients increasingly came from the new middle class, which invested both personal and public funds in buildings that had necessarily to indulge the very taste denounced by connoisseurs. Ivory towers might provide a sanctuary for other-worldly aesthetes; they had little to offer those visual artists who needed to make their mark in the public domain.

Nor was the 'art for art's sake' doctrine a satisfactory answer for those who believed that a love of beautiful things was an essential characteristic of a civilized society. In the visual arts at least, occasional masterpieces might gratify the sensitive few while still compelling them to live among the ugliness of the many. Here the quality of a culture was not to be measured by exceptional works of art but by the degree of beauty that infused all its artefacts and surrounded all its inhabitants. It was to such an ideal state where beauty was the norm that British writers looked back in their reaction to the pervasive ugliness of the Industrial Revolution. For these connoisseurs, the new middle class was not only to be condemned for its lack of taste but for imposing its standards upon society as a whole so that no one, not even artists or aesthetes, could escape its ominous impact.

Unlike the French bourgeoisie, which had achieved political power and was now in a position to indulge those qualities which had brought it success, British manufacturers derived their importance from their economic influence. The horrifying physical and social effects of the Industrial Revolution that ensued incited a line of British writers to turn a disgust for the new unfolding way of life into a critique of a capitalist society. Its architectural application was brilliantly drawn by Pugin. In his book *Contrasts*, two perspectives of a town face each other.[7] The medieval view represents a pastoral scene hallowed by churches, towers, and spires. The illustration of the modern town is dominated by its jail, surrounded by warehouses, dissenting chapels, and a 'socialist hall of science.' The message is plain. The beauty of Gothic architecture was a natural result of a (Catholic) Christian attitude that was pious and humane. The ugliness of modern buildings resulted from the evilness of modern life. This potent, if arbitrary, coupling of design quality with social values became the major argument in the attack on the general standard of taste in nineteenth-century Britain.

Other critics who were more concerned with product design were content to consider the aesthetic dimensions of the problem without tying them to issues of social ethics and political economy. The inferiority of British goods was held generally to be true, and as it was believed that this affected the export market and the ability to compete with foreign imports, the problem had more than purely aesthetic importance. The outcome was that in 1835 the British Parliament set up a committee to investigate the issue of bad design in the manufacturing industries and to make recommendations for its solution.[8]

Ironically, in view of the attacks of French critics on bourgeois taste, the standard against which British designs were being judged was set by the French, whose patterns British manufacturers often pirated. The reason is readily apparent. French taste had been institutionalized since the reign of Louis XIV when the Academy of Painting and Sculpture had been reorganized under the direction of Le

Brun, who had also been put in charge of the Gobelins workshops that supplied the royal furnishings. By the 1830s, when the British parliamentary committee heard from expert witnesses, the French government had secured an acceptable level of design through its numerous schools of design and juried exhibitions of industrial products.

Based on approved values, this policy sustained and preserved a recognized tradition. With designs provided by trained artists, the question whether they were implemented by hand or machine tools turned out to be inconsequential. Production moved easily from the workshop to the factory. Industrialization and mass production were not perceived as problems. Instead, manufacturers of such goods could argue that by multiplying the best designs and making them available to the general public, they were instructing and elevating its taste.[9] Consequently, the French were one step removed from the situation in Britain, where neither an accepted tradition nor a trained body of industrial artists was readily available to manufacturers, who relied for the most part on untrained opinion to fashion what they produced.

It is therefore understandable that the solution recommended by the British parliamentary committee investigating the causes of bad design was to follow the French example for shaping public taste. This included more art galleries (to supplement the National Gallery, which was under construction at the time), more art books and magazines, more art courses in the schools, and a government school of design that was established in London the following year.

Given its acceptance of cultivated taste as the desired norm, the committee had found that it was not just the industrial classes that lacked it. Bad taste was also rampant among the upper class and even affected the graduates of Oxford and Cambridge universities.[10] In other words, virtually everyone except the experts had the wrong sort of taste. But, they pronounced, there was nothing that could not be solved through public education provided by an enlightened authority. It was this view that good taste could be taught and learned that was to confront, confute, and finally assimilate the socio-economic prognosis of Pugin, Ruskin, and Morris.

The first decade of the new School of Design was marked by internal disputes over how to teach design.[11] In this controversy, artists opposed an artistic training, and manufacturers opposed a technical training, each group wanting to protect its own territory. Students were reduced to learning a drawing technique while purportedly refining their visual taste by observing closely the objects that they copied. Nevertheless, by the mid-century, the London school had been supplemented by a number of other schools in the provincial centres, either funded or subsidized by the government, and about fifteen thousand students had graduated from them.[12]

The result was equivocal. Another parliamentary committee concluded that there was no direct evidence to show that the schools had helped to improve the general standard of design of manufactured products, an opinion shared by one of its expert witnesses, Henry Cole.[13] At the same time, Cole was working on the idea of an international exhibition where the quality of British goods could be tested against their foreign competitors.[14]

Cole was both a civil servant and an amateur designer. He had published children's books, marketed the first Christmas card, won a silver medal from the Royal Society of Arts for a popular tea service, set up the firm of Summerly's Art Manufactures to encourage the participation of artists in industry, and, with the painter Richard Redgrave, founded a magazine on design.[15]

Under the patronage of Prince Albert, Cole became a major force behind the Great Exhibition of the Works of Industry of All Nations held in 1851 in the Crystal Palace, and was a member of its executive committee.[16] The exhibition celebrated the success of industrialization and its capacity to provide goods for the new classes it had generated. It showed that factories could manufacture the sort of ornamental articles that once were the sole prerogative of the rich. And it displayed the qualities of design that their manufacturers believed would illustrate the superiority of their products. In doing so, the exhibition marked a unique occasion when the uncurbed taste of the new middle class challenged the authority of aesthetic specialists.

Rather than have the central agency control the selection of the British exhibits, the task was left to nearly 330 separate local committees set up around the country. Their directive was to use their 'knowledge and discretion' to ensure that only 'articles which did honour to our industrial skill as a nation' were included.[17] Manufacturers, with the approval of their peers, responded with products that displayed their ingenuity, invention, and industrial prowess, qualities that, reciprocally, were included among the criteria set down as guidelines for the awards presented by the juries of international experts.[18] Embellishing these works and meeting the requirement of 'beauty of design in form' was a profusion of decorative features emphasizing naturalistic figures and scenes that added a sentimental, moralistic, or fanciful content. Millions of visitors were treated to a display that many would have found a feast for the eyes, engagingly interesting, stimulating to the imagination, and emotionally cheering; a magical presentation of utilitarian objects transformed into household works of art.

The reaction of the leading circle of Britain's professional designers was to denounce the quality of these manufactured products. As their primary instrument of criticism, they employed the idea of fitness or appropriateness, based on abstract reasoning and ethical strictures. Forms should be appropriate to their function. There should be an appropriate use and treatment of materials. Patterns should be appropriate to their application. Motifs should have an appropriate scale. To these were added other prescriptions. There should be no perspective or shadowing on flat surfaces. There should be no discordant colours. There should be no incongruities of subject matter in decorative features. One should not construct ornament but ornament construction. Fitness of purpose and simplicity of result were to be valued over so-called superficial effects.[19]

Perhaps this was a natural response by professionals to the invasion of their sphere of influence by outsiders. Interestingly, the effect the exhibition had on the architectural theory of the day was the reverse in the case of the novel iron-and-glass structure of the Crystal Palace, which observed the edicts of the Cole circle. The invention of an untrained self-made man, Joseph Paxton, the design for the Crystal Palace itself was dismissed as being only suitable for utilitarian buildings by architects who continued to imitate historical styles.

The reaction of Cole and his associates could also have been the result of seeing the mass dissemination of a style that had once been the preserve of the cultivated class. The handles, spouts, and lids of both Cole's own teapot design, and one created for him by Redgrave, had been ornamented just like those that were later censured.[20] More specifically, the shift in taste might have stemmed from Redgrave's own resolve to develop a consistent theory to inform his lectures at the School of Design to which he had been appointed in 1847. By attempting to reveal the essential characteristics of design, rather than striving to explain the actual diversity of it, Redgrave was led to concentrate on a limited set of admissible qualities and to reject those that did not fit into his narrow logic. Whatever the cause, by the end of the Great Exhibition, Cole's associates had formulated their position as to what they considered good design, and this excluded most of the exhibits.

This codification of design must have appealed to Cole, who, as an accomplished administrator, would have welcomed a systematic method of defining and promulgating the principles of such a potentially arbitrary subject. The object, of course, had long been achieved in architectural design education at the École des Beaux-Arts. Cole's opportunity to implement a comparable system came immediately after the Great Exhibition, in 1852, when he was appointed to head a new government Department of Practical Art within the Board of Trade – later the art section of the Department of Science and Art under the Education Department – with Redgrave as his artistic deputy.

By the time of Cole's appointment, the original school of design had been supplemented by twenty more in the major manufacturing towns. But for the new administrators, there was little point in securing well-designed products if there was no one with the discernment to buy them. With the intention 'of laying the foundation for correct judgment, both in the consumer and the producer,' Cole initiated a comprehensive program intended to educate the entire British public.[21] This strategy was to become the standard response of design specialists to the challenge to their status presented by interests and opinions other than their own.

As a guide for public taste, selected items were purchased from the Great Exhibition and put on display in the department's offices to illustrate the 'true' principles of design. Prominent among these good examples were articles from the East India Company, which the Cole faction particularly admired. Reinforcing the message was another small exhibit exposing products designed on 'false' principles – although this was soon dismantled after their manufacturers complained.[22]

It was this display that provoked the satire 'A House Full of Horrors,'[23] published in Dickens' *Household Words*. In this cautionary tale, a once contented man pays a visit to the exhibit and is shocked to discover that the world is full of bad taste, including his own. From then on his life is miserable. Upset by pagodas on wallpaper and tigers on rugs, he finally has a nervous breakdown when he sees the butterfly that decorates the inside of his empty cup. If the Cole group took its newly acquired precepts seriously, the educated middle class was not necessarily ready to accept its point of view.

Disregarding any resistance, Cole's drive was inexorable. The department's first purchases formed the nucleus of the collection that achieved world renown as the Victoria and Albert Museum. The principal School of Design moved nearby to become subsequently the Royal College of Art, and by the time of Cole's retirement in 1873, the number of provincial schools under the department's jurisdiction had increased sixfold.[24]

Simultaneously, the department inaugurated a long-term program to instil its own values and taste in the working class. During the mid-1800s, the government subsidized schools set up by religious-based philanthropic organizations to instruct the poor. Cole offered to supply these schools with approved models from nature, art, and industry, and arranged to train teachers in their use. Children were expected to learn their merit by assiduously copying them, so that drawing became the instrument to mould a new generation capable of appreciating the aesthetic principles that the Cole faction claimed to have uncovered. With the enactment of a universal state system of elementary education in 1870, the number of schools under government jurisdiction increased dramatically, and by the end of the century, more than two million children were receiving organized instruction in the subject of art.[25]

The result was a total failure relative to its aims. The impact of this massive attempt at education (or indoctrination) of the buying public in the matter of taste turned out to be indiscernible to the eyes of future aesthetic specialists. A lifetime later, it was as if nothing had happened. A new government Council for Art and Industry, established in 1934, presented the same arguments and the same answers: the need for enlightened consumers, and the solution of more art education, better teachers, even the supply of well-designed objects for the children to study.[26] Only the official taste had changed.

The council urged local education authorities to improve the design of their schools, providing illustrations of classrooms in a Modern idiom. Overlooked was the merit of earlier buildings, which – like those erected by the London School Board – had been model examples for their time and which were preserved by an even later generation as part of its architectural heritage. As for design instruction itself, the medium of imitation was to give way to the goal of imagination.[27] The notion that a close study of selected objects would lead to the recognition of universal principles of design was simply abandoned, and replaced by the equally speculative contention that the encouragement of their own artistic expression would enable children subsequently to appreciate it in other people's designs.

For both generations of aesthetic reformers who sought to correct the situation through education, the problem was straightforward: there was an objective quality called good taste, and therefore it could be taught. They had no sense that there were any deeper issues involved. This position was left to William Morris, who invoked the theory that linked art to society.[28]

Twenty-six years younger than Cole, Morris was only seventeen at the time of the Great Exhibition. When he married in 1859, he looked for suitable furnishings for his new home and, finding nothing to his taste, decided to market his own line of decorative arts.[29] His firm soon came to be known for its stained glass windows and furniture, while Morris' own specialties included tapestries, textiles, carpets, and wallpapers.[30] Yet his endeavours of the next decades ultimately brought disillusionment. In 1875, Cole was knighted for his services to the state. By that time, Morris had almost arrived at the opposite conclusion – that any improvements were impossible under the prevailing economic conditions – and later openly declared himself a socialist.

Morris' reasoning owed much to Ruskin and, by extension, to Pugin. The idea that bad societies produce bad art had been simple, effective, and quick to take hold. On one side was pictured the materialistic, grasping entrepreneur, interested only in wealth and its display; on the other side, the vast new working class whose natural sensitivity had been debased and brutalized by factory conditions. The cause: machine production, which had destroyed the crafts and thereby broken the ritual bond between the people and their artefacts. As Ruskin put it in *The Stones of Venice*, 'We have much studied and much perfected, of late, the great civilized invention of the division of labour; only we give it a false name. It is not, truly speaking, the labour that is divided; but the men.'[31]

According to this line of reasoning, by severing the traditional connection between labourers and their handiwork, the Industrial Revolution had turned them from creative workers into mechanical operatives. Whereas in a craft society, all artefacts were instinctively embodied with the artisan's innate sense of beauty, machine-made products were void of any artistic significance. Reflecting what manufacturers hoped would sell in a competitive market, they catered to the basest appetites of human nature. Broken by the monotony and harshness of employment in the factories, mills, and mines, and surrounded by ugliness, workers were only too likely to seek consolation in spurious substitutes. These the new breed of manufacturers was anxious to supply. Often themselves having risen by their own energy and ruthlessness, they had only contempt for non-materialistic values and by the power they wielded imposed their own standards on the people they oppressed.

Morris' contributions to politics, literature, and design have been widely honoured, and may be taken for granted. But there were also many contradictions between theory and practice in his life.[32] He started out by intending to provide beautiful artefacts for the public at large, and ended up catering to the rich. He preached socialism and equality, but earned a great deal more than his own employees and reasoned that no good purpose would be served in sharing his income with them.[33] Following Ruskin, he argued that art was the expression of the workers' joy in their labour, but expected his workers to follow his designs no matter how tedious and repetitive they might be. He denounced the debilitating effects of mechanical production, but subcontracted work to factories that used the most technologically advanced power-driven looms.[34]

Morris' distortions went even deeper. The artistry of his products might possibly be the result of the pleasure he took in his work, but this participation in the creative act was not allowed to his clients, who accepted what they were offered or went without.[35] Nor was there anything new in this relationship between artist and patron. Certainly the male half of the patron or client class had seldom created its own household objects. The design of public buildings especially, against which Morris raged, had always been the responsibility of a professional group of architects. And if earlier vernacular housing seemed to sensitized contemporary eyes to be less ugly than their own, even that was not because its occupants had built it themselves. Construction had long been the domain of specialized trades.

At most, any pleasure that purchasers had in good craftsmanship was vicarious, the joy that was taken in someone else's capabilities. It followed that if the moneyed class could have its aesthetic needs supplied by a special set of artists employing craftspeople to carry out their instructions, the working class ought to be able to enjoy the same advantages by encouraging artists to utilize industrial processes and the cost-reduction benefits of mass production.

This resolution to the problem was outside Morris' philosophy. He condemned the division of society into producers and consumers but still contributed to it. His position was not shared by Ruskin, who believed that artistic talent was rare and that the public's role was to learn to recognize and appreciate it; that it was his calling to awaken the moral virtues and artistic sensibilities of his readers, not so that they would produce art, but that they might enrich their lives through its experience.

This conviction led Ruskin to denounce Cole and his associates for their claim that they could teach students to design.[36] In contrast, Morris' contention was that in a decent society human beings would naturally be artistic; that is, all would be more or less like him, but instead of having to sell their goods, they would participate freely in their exchange and enjoyment.[37]

Morris maintained that the Industrial Revolution had made art in his own time impossible, even though his friends included the painter Edward Burne-Jones and the architect Webb, and he had many art-world contemporaries in countries where commercialization and industrialization had taken place. Focusing on the decorative arts and architecture, he declared that they had been ruined by machine production and the materialistic ethic that accompanied it.

This assertion that others, unconstrained by circumstances, would share his idea of beauty, was another example of the reformer's skill in linking disparate ideas and drawing arbitrary (if extremely influential) connections between them. Morris' taste was not widely shared by his educated associates from outside the realm of design. The actual situation was caricatured by George Bernard Shaw, who quipped that one of the reasons Morris had not joined the socialist Fabian Society was that he loathed the ugliness of the furnishings in the suburban houses where its members met.[38]

The essential difference between the articles bought by the (unenlightened) middle class and the working class was not basically a matter of appearance. It was more a question of materials, workmanship, and cost. The chimney ornament in a working-class home was mostly a cruder version of its porcelain counterpart. 'Educated' design was thought to be something essentially different and 'superior.' Although it was not readily apparent from their behaviour towards one another, the competing aesthetic factions of the times shared a similar taste. While Ruskin despised Cole, whose magazine had once criticized the design of the book cover of the first edition of *The Seven Lamps of Architecture*,[39] Morris accepted an important commission from Cole to decorate the Green Dining Room at the South Kensington (Victoria and Albert) Museum.

Similarly, Morris in theory repudiated the 'art for art's sake' philosophy associated with the painter J. McNeill Whistler. But outside observers saw little difference between his furnishings and the interior design of the London home of Whistler's friend, the architect E.W. Godwin, who had Ellen Terry wear a blue kimono to match the décor of their drawing-room, which was centred around a full-size cast of the Venus de Milo wreathed in incense smoke.[40]

It was Godwin (afterwards replaced by Richard Norman Shaw) who designed the first houses for the model London garden suburb of Bedford Park, which became a fashionable place of residence for 'refined' middle-class families who, to cite a contemporary account, had cultivated tastes but moderate means.[41] In their reception rooms, Morris wallpapers might fittingly supply the backdrop to 'art' furniture and Japanese porcelain.[42] Consequently, when the hero in Gilbert and Sullivan's *Patience* came to mock aesthetes, he did not distinguish between the Pre-Raphaelites and Impressionists, or between medievalism and the fad for Japanese art and design. The Cole faction's emphasis on design precepts, the Arts and Crafts movement's insistence on the need to return to design essentials, the personal creativity of Morris himself and of architects like Godwin and Shaw – all infused by the moral exhortations of Ruskin and Morris – had culminated in a new style with which to confront the 'philistines.'

From the standpoint of its advocates, this could be viewed as a benevolent act of fostering 'good' taste in order to make the citizenry more 'civilized.' However, the possession of 'good' taste could also be seen as a mark of superiority in the ranking order of society. Aesthetes prior to the Industrial Revolution had regarded taste as an upper-class property. Nineteenth-century reformers ostensibly wanted to share it – but only on their own terms and to their own advantage.

Those who subscribed to 'good' taste could use it to distinguish themselves from the ever-increasing middle class to which most of them now belonged. By asserting their own special status, they could then claim that they had the right (and duty) to be taken as the ideal standard against which the rest of the population should be judged. The effect was to entrench a form of prejudice that devalued everyone else and allowed its perpetrators to exercise the sort of psychological dominance that had once been part of the wider impact of aristocratic power.

Thus in terms of product sales, the 'cultivated' set lost its battle against the 'bad' design of ordinary merchandise and would continue to rail bitterly against it. But within the more ambiguous dynamics of social influence, it was extremely successful in getting itself recognized as a legitimate authority, and was thereby enabled to exercise considerable power in formulating social attitudes. In this area, its victory was so complete that even those it denounced came to believe that it represented the ideal of true 'culture,' which, unfortunately, was beyond their reach.

Pugin had contended that nineteenth-century society was bad and therefore produced bad architecture. Morris had come to the same conclusion that good design could never be widely accepted, because the capitalist system of competitive commerce made this impossible. Both men had assumed that their own aesthetic standards were objectively right and universally valid, and tied their lack of popular success to the social, economic, and political conditions under which they lived. In particular, they laid the blame on the spiritual short-comings of the materialistic middle class. And it was this interpreta-tion of events that was carried into the twentieth century by other writers with a similar outlook and intent.

By viewing the new era of industrialization and urbanization in negative terms, British designers and critics made it impossible for themselves to take advantage of the new style they had created. By the end of the century, the Industrial Revolution had consolidated its control of the means of production, and the division of labour was about to enter an even more advanced phase with the introduction of the assembly line. Unable to accept that what it had achieved had any place in this new world, the British movement shortly came to an end with a series of rural houses.[43] Its theory, however, was soon to be adopted and rearranged by others elsewhere, so that industrial-ization was given a positive value, and individual creativity was denied in favour of an 'objective' style that could be claimed to be outside class values.

Formed in Germany in 1907, the Werkbund brought together artists, manufacturers, and merchants in the cause of improving the quality of manufactured goods.[44] Its principal organizer was the government official and architect Hermann Muthesius, who had been greatly influenced by the British Arts and Crafts movement, which he had closely observed as a cultural attaché in London. Like the Cole circle before him, Muthesius insisted that rules were implicit in the facts of design, production, and marketing; that an article's use, the nature of the materials to be employed, the techniques of the manufacturing process, and the economics of supply and demand would, left to their own internal logic, generate their own design solution. This claim was rounded off by the appeal to a mystical notion of form that, in embodying the spirit of each age, was both its motivating ideal and, subsequently, its symbol. The Greeks had created the temple, the eighteenth century the princely salon. The modern age must necessarily have its own 'type-form,' which would give spiritual meaning to the realities of its situation and ennoble the commonplace to the status of art.[45]

Muthesius' position did not go unchallenged. It was opposed at the Werkbund meeting of 1914 by the Belgian Henry van de Velde, one of the originators of Art Nouveau and an artistic presence in Weimar for thirteen years. Van de Velde rejected any restrictions on artistic imagination and argued that a valid style for the age could only emerge from individuals following their own creative impulse. But the combination of common sense and metaphysics espoused by Muthesius proved irresistible. All the ingredients for a credible ideology now fell into place. The scenario seemed perfect. Industrialization, once considered the curse of the nineteenth century, was understood as its most notable characteristic. Factories were its type-form expression – in a remarkable reversal that took them from the bottom of the architectural hierarchy of building types to the top. The output from them would spread its benefits around the world, each well-designed product both a symbol of its era and an object of beauty, the one derived from the other. Design was no longer to be dependent on the vagaries of creative artists but an expression of the spirit of the age. Human creativity, the essence of Morris' social and artistic philosophy – and the measure of the Art Nouveau and Secession movements – was now condemned as unhealthy individualism by his nominal followers.

For in this revised line of reasoning, artists did not invent styles for themselves or others. Styles were generated by deep-seated social, or even spiritual, conditions that manifested themselves in 'art-form'. The role of architects and designers was to allow this 'will-to-form' to materialize, to uncover it, to help it on its way. In embodying the abstract essence of its civilization, design was no longer a matter of taste, of arbitrary notions of beauty, but of truth to objective laws.

Gone were all the doubts that nineteenth-century critics had turned into a denunciation of the capitalist system. Admittedly at one level, much had improved. The overall standard of existence had risen for manual workers, and their working and living conditions were undeniably better. The older, brutal *laissez-faire* system was slowly giving way to a more enlightened form of capitalism, which took some aspects of the workers' welfare into account, even if usually only for reasons of self-interest. But in a more fundamental sense, the situation had not changed at all. From the Ruskin-Morris standpoint, the essential values of capitalism remained materialistic. Workers were still doing mind-dulling routine jobs, they had no say in the products they made, and there was no real cause to take pleasure in their work.

The new German theorists had looked at the same facts as their British predecessors and turned the older interpretation of them upside down, converting a negative critique into a positive endorsement. In this updated reading of events, the Industrial Revolution was not a tragedy but a success. Factories were not squalid structures but symbols of their age. Workers were not demoralized by mass production techniques but proud of being associated with the power of their machines. As for art and design, they did not have to exist artificially outside society, but were a legitimate expression of it. And once again the argument used by Cole was put forward by the Werkbund: that to raise the level of public taste to appreciate the quality of the goods its members produced, all that was needed was education. For now manufacturers were also to be convinced that the specialist's notion of design would not only bring them international prestige but also increased sales.

What was this design? Essentially, an extension of the proscriptions and practices of the nineteenth-century aesthetic reformers. As in the early years of the British move towards an authoritative set of design principles, there was initially considerable disagreement and variation among the participants, except that they all endorsed 'quality' goods. Over the following two decades, however, the most vocal faction stressed characteristics similar to – though finally even more exclusive than – those that had been advocated half a century before; that is, abstract form and pattern, enlivened by a not too obvious infusion of personal creativity. Moreover, a major manufacturer was already having these characteristics injected directly into the process of mass production through the paid intervention of a professional artist.

Established a generation earlier to exploit the new market for electrical power, the German firm A.E.G. had grown quickly into a vast industrial enterprise. In 1907, its design program was placed under the direction of Peter Behrens, who had been a painter and was then director of the school of arts and crafts in Düsseldorf, a position obtained for him by Muthesius.[46] His new assignment was to be responsible for the design of a wide range of graphics, products, and buildings. Providing designs that were sufficiently impersonal in appearance but with more than a touch of fashionable elegance, Behrens became the foremost example of the Werkbund ideal of using industry to cultivate society.

What Behrens began, his recent assistants Walter Gropius and Adolf Meyer completed. With their Fagus Factory of 1911, they took the Arts and Crafts vernacular concept and updated it, creating what came to be viewed as the image of an objective architecture seemingly formed by the functional, technical, economic, and social forces of an industrial rather than craft-based era. Appointed director of the Bauhaus school of design following World War I, Gropius – after some early vacillation – was instrumental in extending the scope of the new style to encompass all design applications.[47] Given aesthetic support through its association with contemporary art styles, and extensively promoted by its few, but articulate, advocates – not least the Bauhaus itself, which devised its own advertising expertise – the style, soon to be labelled Modern, was ultimately adopted by professional designers and architects around the world.

Whereas previous styles could be viewed as the preserve of the educated class, the Modern style was explicitly linked to the working class through its use for low income housing. During the nineteenth-century phase of industrialization in Britain, the architectural profession, and in particular its stylistic leaders, had been noticeably absent from the ranks of the reformers who had attempted to alleviate its most harmful effects.[48] Trained to offer their art to those who could afford to pay for it, they had shown little interest in the plight of their social inferiors.

The architects who produced plans in the latter part of the century for such model communities as those erected for the workers of the Lever brothers at Port Sunlight and the Cadburys at Bournville were exceptions and unknown. Similarly, it was a would-be reformer, Ebenezer Howard, who in 1898 published his idea for the formation of new towns to reduce the overcrowding of existing cities and to rehouse the inhabitants of their slums in a way that would combine the best features of town and country living. Five years later, Letchworth became Britain's first garden city, planned by Raymond Unwin and Barry Parker, disciples of Morris' theories.[49]

These developments were noted by Muthesius in his comprehensive book *Das englische Haus*, published in two editions in Germany in the decade before World War I.[50] The provision of housing for the working class in Germany had roughly followed its evolution in England.[51] Most was supplied by private enterprise, and without adequate government regulation, produced the same objectionable conditions. By the 1890s, however, a number of benevolent societies were attempting to improve the standard of low-rental housing, and in this undertaking they were aided by the architectural profession including some of its leading members. Alfred Messel was on the committee of a housing association in Berlin and designed blocks of apartments for it. Muthesius contributed to the theory – and practice – of cottage estates. This reform process accelerated after the debacle of World War I and the swing towards socialist ideals that followed it. The Weimar Republic encouraged housing construction through the public ownership of land and the provision of capital at reduced interest rates,[52] and in the years before the impact of the Great Depression, half the new housing erected in Germany was financed with public funds.[53]

By taking a conspicuous role in this activity, the proponents of the Modern style quickly assumed the role of technical experts, which allowed them to apply their style to working class estates and, by extension, to claim that they were able to design society as a whole. That the working class was not only superior in numbers but also in value was commonly believed by both communists and socialists. The Russian Revolution, therefore, gave the idea material support. The same idea, however, had been previously absorbed as a by-product of the professional regard for the Arts and Crafts movement.

Fortified by their idealized view of the Middle Ages, both Ruskin and Morris had made the condition of the manual worker central to their thesis. From their perspective, the working class was intrinsically noble because it made things with its hands, as opposed to the new middle class which was only concerned with making money. Both men had looked on the working class as the main instrument for the recovery of civilization. Ruskin, who was paternalistic in outlook, had wanted it to accept its given role under the guidance of enlightened leaders, and to find contentment and self-respect in the perfection of its duties.[54] Morris had dismissed the idea that the capitalist system would ever allow its leaders to do more than trifle with the appalling conditions it had generated, and asserted that any significant change would have to stem from the workers themselves. Morris also reversed the social ideal. Believing that the creation of beauty was a natural activity that would be revived once the populace had been liberated from the evil effects of capitalism, Morris contended that society as a whole – even the existing upper classes – would benefit under the new order when everyone had fulfilled themselves by becoming manual workers.

These two positions, of generalizing the working class as a social ideal, and of arrogating the paternalistic role of acting as its leader and guide, were merged by the advocates of the Modern style. Initially, in Germany, this idea was projected through the prism of that country's background of philosophical mysticism concerning the relationship of the group to a higher authority. Its historical representation was the Gothic cathedral towering over the medieval dwellings below, an image brought up to date by Bruno Taut, in which the spirit of the people was apotheosized in crystal form through the visionary activity of the inspired architect.[55]

But without the endorsement of any powerful element of society, such architectural ideas were merely exercises in artistic expression. Having attempted, and failed, to gain direct control over a major sector of architectural production, their proponents, like Gropius and Taut, turned to a more materialistic explanation of their aims, better suited to the political situation in Germany, which was becoming normalized. They recast their work as the embodiment of the spirit of the age, rather than of the nation, and redefined the agrarian *Volk* as the industrialized working-class mass, which became the target of the architect's idealism.

The substitution proved successful. By the end of the 1920s, the proponents of the Modern style had displaced their garden-city predecessors as the professional advocates of social concern. One of this group, Ernst May, who had worked in Parker and Unwin's office before World War I, was subsequently appointed city architect for Frankfurt, where fifteen thousand dwellings were erected between 1925 and 1933 in estates containing churches, schools, and other community facilities.[56] During a similar period, Taut held the position of chief architect for the Berlin subsidiary of GEHAG, an organization set up by working-class unions to erect housing for its members, which was responsible for more than nine thousand dwellings.[57] Also in Berlin, Gropius joined Hans Scharoun and others to design the various blocks in the Siemensstadt estate, after carrying out similar commissions in Dessau and Karlsruhe.

The architects of the Modern style were certainly not alone in designing low-rental housing. Many other units were built in a vernacular, traditional, or romantic style. For example, the architects of London County Council produced forty thousand dwellings at the same time as May and Taut, and double that number in the period between the two world wars, all in a conservative brick idiom applied to blocks of flats and cottage estates.[58] None the less, the linkage between the Modern style and a modern (interpreted as 'better') way of life was both easy to argue and to be believed. As the American sociologist, Catherine Bauer, explained it, both practical and aesthetic solutions seemed to stem from the same contemporary conditions.[59]

The idea was emphasized through the appropriation of the English term 'modern,' which replaced the German word for 'new.' In 1929 both Taut and Hitchcock wrote books entitled *Modern Architecture*. With proselytizing zeal, the recently founded Museum of Modern Art published its catalogue in 1932 under two titles, *Modern Architecture* and *Modern Architects*, to augment an exhibition that was mounted to promote the style. Bauer's *Modern Housing* appeared in 1934; F.R.S. Yorke's *The Modern House* and, with F. Gibberd, *The Modern Flat*, in 1934 and 1937. By 1936 there was Pevsner's *Pioneers of the Modern*

Movement, and in 1937, W.C. Behrendt's *Modern Building*. Conversely, the difficulty faced by anyone else who tried to claim that their work was equally, or more, expressive of the contemporary world, became evident when Wright also called his collection of lectures on his own beliefs, *Modern Architecture*, but felt forced to refute the pronouncements of his European contemporaries.[60]

For the admirers of the Modern style, the German housing projects possessed health-giving qualities. Their parallel blocks of simple geometric forms seemed to embrace sun, light, air, and greenery, and promised a new era for their working class inhabitants.[61] Enthusing over Otto Haesler, whose early work at Celle had led to this new low-rental housing type, Philip Johnson announced that he was probably the foremost housing architect in the world.[62] Others questioned the supposed logic of the Modern style in which these housing estates were designed. The aging Muthesius pointed out that it was 'somewhat amusing to note that the representatives of cubic constructions deceive themselves into believing that their creations are purely constructive and economic and that they have nothing to do with art.'[63] It was this art of basic geometric forms that was to become the aesthetic taste of the next generation of architects and designers, to be applied to everything from a desk lamp to the city.

In prescribing the type of housing to be occupied by the working class, architects had various motives. Some acted from compassion and a sense of responsibility. Others treated the design of housing as an expedient extension of their normal practice. A few believed it was their calling to tell people how they ought to live. Probably most, if not all, of them had good intentions. This activity was now to be generalized and applied to society as a whole. A project for an 'Industrial City' had been developed previously by Tony Garnier and published in 1917.[64] This was based on socialistic ideals and was similar in size to Howard's garden-city proposal, being planned for thirty-five thousand inhabitants. Five years later, Le Corbusier expanded this concept of total design into a complete 'Contemporary City' for three million inhabitants, and proposed that it be governed by a ruling élite, which would include not only captains of industry and business but also poets and artists.[65]

His grandiose ideas were quickly taken up by other advocates of the Modern style. The first study sessions of their organization, CIAM, had dealt with the 'minimum dwelling'; the second, with 'rational lot division.' Both issues were related to the immediate practical problem of designing acceptable housing for the least cost. The third meeting, in 1933, took 'the functional city' as the architects' realm, and declared, 'Architecture holds the key to everything'.[66]

The proposition that they were 'planners' was very appealing to architects and was speedily incorporated into their mythology. 'The whole world is out of joint through lack of planning,' announced the president of the Royal Institute of British Architects in 1934. Luckily, the architect was 'the one person in the community trained to plan,' so the rest of the community should learn to appreciate and follow the architect's advice.[67] In this way, architects came to convince themselves that their area of competence encompassed the whole built environment and, by extension, everybody who inhabited it. For many of them, the social ramifications of their work were hidden in the assumption that they were simply exercising their technical skills and aesthetic taste. For others, the connection was used as further evidence of the importance of their mission.

This move to assume responsibility for the total design of cities could be viewed as the logical next step in the attainment of an earlier ideal of extending art to encompass all life. Alternatively, it could be seen as the attempt of a small clique to impose its doctrinaire beliefs on society as a whole. Whatever the motivation, it had important implications concerning the relationship between art and society.

Previously, aesthetes had drawn a line between art and popular taste. The former had been associated with the educated élite, the latter with the uncultivated mass. Both, however, continued to coexist so that all groups could enjoy their own symbolic fare. Music, dance, literature, sculpture: each had its art and popular forms. The specialists in these fields had never attempted to take over or eliminate their parallel alternatives. Designers of 'well-designed' products, for example, did not expect to have their 'tasteless' competitors prohibited.

Architects were now attempting to erase this division in the art that was most public in its impact. By becoming involved in mass housing and the detailed design of entire towns, the profession was in effect undertaking to exclude people generally from exercising choice in the design of their own everyday world.

Architects might see this as a service to society. But because of their privileged position as a profession, the actual result was to impose their professional values on a public that lacked the means to protect its own interests. From the public's perspective, this could be considered incongruous, considering that architects, in theory, owed their professional privileges to it, through the enactment of laws by its representatives in government.

While the idea of designing entire cities was old, the size, scope, and, most important, the feasibility of actually constructing such utopian visions, were new. Following the lead of Le Corbusier, architects could now project the image of the ideal environment that might be achieved if left to their expert control. In turn, government authorities were willing to accept their claims because they were members of an approved profession. This assumption of power by architects peaked in the many new towns erected in Europe after World War II. There, the total environment, sometimes down to its litter bins, was pre-designed by the dominant professional set, so that residents were forced to retreat into their dwelling units before they could indulge their own preferences.

Obviously, in a free-enterprise system, the considerable inroads achieved by architects could not be equalled by product designers. Manufacturers had to compete in the marketplace and necessarily had to take the interests of their potential customers into account. Neither could the same success be realized where large components of towns (especially their residential areas) were subject to similar considerations. In these the divisions between trained and untrained taste evident in the nineteenth century continued, and the specialists could only fall back on their established tradition of condemning all other tastes but their own. Once again, they used the middle class as the focus for their attack.

Adapted to twentieth-century conditions, the old theme took on new characteristics. Nineteenth-century critics had castigated the middle class for being mercenary and vulgar. The new indictment condemned it for being shallow and boring, and argued that it would reduce everything to its own level of mediocrity.[68] In Britain, the domicile of the middle class was a scaled-down version of the Queen Anne house, with bay windows, pebble dash (rough stucco), and sometimes, applied timbering, fronted by a small garden that was entered through a wooden gate framing the motif of a rising sun.[69] Purchased by the tens of thousands in the interwar years, these were an affront to the current generation of British architects, who had left Queen Anne behind and whose updated preference for plain rectangular concrete blocks of flats was only realized later. But by that time the industrialized world had divided into two political spheres, and nineteenth-century notions of class took different directions under the opposing systems.

The pre–World War II advocates of the Modern style had contended that it best served the needs of the working class which was their standard for the new mass society. In the postwar era, the population of the Eastern bloc under Communist rule continued to be largely working class but, under Stalin's dictate, the buildings designed for it were generally either in a traditional style or 'functional' without any compensating artistic pretence. In contrast, the people of the Western bloc of nations were engulfed by buildings in a Modern style during a postwar period of prosperity in which middle class attitudes became the norm.

Although the architects of the Modern style had achieved considerable success in disseminating their views, they had actually been responsible for relatively few buildings erected during the interwar years. The typical architectural style in Western countries at this time tended to be either traditional or, if 'contemporary,' more ornamental than Modern. World War II and the defeat of Germany dramatically altered this situation. The traditional styles sanctioned by the Nazi regime were discredited by association with it, and condemned as 'reactionary,' even though they had been equally favoured by architects and governments in democratic nations. Conversely, the belief that the Modern style implied social as well as artistic reform inspired a new generation of architects who had come of age during a period of reduced opportunities due to the Great Depression and the war.

While the Modern style had also included expensive houses and

apartments, and even commercial skyscrapers – such as the Philadelphia Saving Fund Society building by Howe and Lescaze – it had
been heralded as the means by which a new way of life would be
attained by society as a whole, free from the bourgeois distortions of
the earlier capitalist era. In this vision there was an implicit assumption that the masses would exclude the stereotypical middle class that
had previously eluded and threatened the aesthetes' control. The new
industrial or machine-age 'society' that architects envisaged as the
beneficiary of their wisdom was an abstract concept that admitted
only grateful inhabitants and ignored any dissenting elements.

Instead of disappearing, however, the middle class was about to
become a major influence in Western nations. This shift in class
attitudes undercut the mythical alliance between an altruistic architectural profession and a deserving (if ignorant) populace. The very
class that had always been used as a butt to ridicule, and as a compelling reason for the need of professional control, now saw its own
values widely adopted.

The main victor of the war and the wealthiest nation in the world,
the United States initially provided the most advanced example of
this development. Heralded by the sociologist C. Wright Mills, a new
white-collar class had emerged from the old working class to dominate the social scene, nourished by the traditional American ideal of
equality, and brought into existence by the successful advance of
capitalism.[70] In a poll carried out in 1940, *Fortune* magazine inquired
how persons would name the class to which they belonged. The
results were reported in a table headed 'The U.S. Is Middle Class,'
which showed that nearly half of the respondents saw themselves as
part of the middle-class spectrum.[71] Furthermore, when pressed, even
the majority of the wealthy and the poor considered that they
belonged within it. Specialists were to argue over the validity and
significance of these findings, but most agreed that Americans generally perceived themselves to be outside the traditional European
class system that emphasized the importance of the working class.

The component of this new expanded middle class that Mills
analysed was its office employees. The old labour force, Mills argued,
had produced goods; the mid-twentieth-century labour force
coordinated, serviced, and distributed them. Its work habitat was the

office building, its residential habitat was the suburb, and its characteristics and behaviour were to provoke a frenzied reaction from social critics. The tone of the response was set by books like William H. Whyte's *The Organization Man*, which changed the American image from the free-wheeling Yankee individualist to the corporate man in the grey flannel suit.[72] Even a 'liberal' critic like Lewis Mumford, frustrated by having his advice ignored by those he thought it his mission to save, forgot his humanitarianism and portrayed the families living in suburbs as a homogeneous, conformist mass watching the same television programs while eating the same frozen dinners; a class that was to be pitied, if not condemned, for the shallowness of its relationships and interests, and the dulling mediocrity of its taste.[73]

Predictably, its replacement of the working class as the main component of Western society was received by the art world with the same hostility that had marked its initial rise to prominence a century before. Writing as early as 1939 in *Partisan Review*, Clement Greenberg poured scorn on the 'kitsch' that was 'the epitome of all that is spurious in the life of our times,' a statement often reprinted during the next decades.[74] Others, like Dwight Macdonald, suggested new pejorative terms such as 'masscult' to mock the general population's aesthetic values.[75] 'Intellectuals,' who might have been expected to be committed to the disinterested search for knowledge, became ardent defenders of their own tastes.

Art-world theorists had often overlooked the defects of the working class in their assumption that these would disappear as its external conditions improved. They failed to foresee that a rising standard of living would induce people to have middle-class expectations even when they held working-class jobs. Labelled by one economist as the 'golden age' of advanced capitalism, the quarter of a century after World War II brought an unprecedented period of prosperity to the Western world.[76] This, in turn, altered the way people thought of themselves in terms of class.[77] The extent of this change was marked by two Italian films, produced forty years apart. Vittorio de Sica's *The Bicycle Thief*, shown in 1948, was a classic work of social realism that expressed the anguish of working-class life at the time. By 1989, in Maurizio Nichetti's *The Icicle Thief*, similar scenes could be manipu-

lated in a satire of contemporary consumerism because they looked
as if they came from the archives of another era.

Not only incomes increased dramatically. So did educational levels.
For example, in the United States between 1940 and 1970, the median
number of completed school years doubled while the proportion of
university degrees granted, tripled.[78] The 'masses' who once had just
enough money and education to cope with everyday existence had
become an affluent and knowledgeable society. This burgeoning
middle class represented a world of ordinary people who were less
than perfect, with common human traits including the desire to
shape their own way of life rather than to have it decided for them.
It was this quality of ordinariness that offended the art-world set,
which considered itself special and superior, and its work profound.
Art, in these terms, explored the realm of the spirit – not the ordinary human spirit, but its transcendental state. Seemingly unable to
recognize, reach out to, or embrace this epiphany of meaning, the
new middle class community was dismissed as contemptible by its
art-world adversaries.

Although it had long since been dropped by aesthetic reformers,
possibly the earlier dogma survived – that the working class did, or
made, things with its hands (even though they were used mainly to
operate machines), whereas the middle class applied its mind or its
(largely female) manual skills to administration and sales. More
likely, only the animosity towards commerce remained, which artists
found repugnant (except where it affected their own sales or commissions). In that case, there was no potential emancipation of the
middle class to allow the possibility of a more fulfilling way of life.

These beliefs were so embedded in the mythology of the world of
art that they could even be used to explain away its own shifts of
fashion. Having demonized the middle class, critics could then
denounce outmoded styles by linking them to it. New York's Lever
House, designed by Skidmore, Owings, and Merrill, provided an
instructive example.[79] Honoured on its completion in 1952 by the
American Institute of Architects, it was praised by critics at the time
for the logic, clarity, and elegance of its form. Subsequently it was to
appear in most architectural histories as the definitive mid-twentieth-
century statement of the Modern style, as well as providing a model

for other office buildings in various parts of the world. As time passed by, however, and a new art-world set wanted to discredit their older, and more successful, competitors, these qualities were ignored and the building was denounced by association with its use. Located near Madison Avenue, the centre of the advertising industry, Lever House was branded as a metaphor for corporate America, its hollow image nothing more than the packaging of another consumer product for the commercial exploitation of a soulless society.

The falseness of this argument was underlined when a similar glass-and-metal box was designed by one of the art world's heroes, Ludwig Mies van der Rohe (in collaboration with Johnson) and built across the road for Seagram Company. Furthermore, the following decades saw an accelerating collusion between the art world and its corporate clients, who exploited it as an advertising medium. But by this time architects had lost interest in justifying their work in socio-economic terms and had rediscovered that the pursuit of 'art for art's sake' was both more exciting and rewarding.

Even here, the bourgeois theme was exploited in a specious way to excuse yet another turn in architectural taste while defending its legitimacy against any encroachment by outsiders. Caught up in the accelerating trend of public opposition to the massive demolition operations of the postwar years, architects began to abandon their demand for a Modern style and to proclaim the importance of a community's architectural heritage. This move was ratified by Johnson in 1978 when, as one of the profession's chief taste-makers, he designed (in partnership with John Burgee) the headquarters building of the AT&T Corporation. From one perspective, this was just another skyscraper on a congested Manhattan site. Its uniqueness resided in its 'Chippendale' parapet.[80] Historical motifs became the latest architectural fad. Favoured by middle-class home buyers, such additions were derided as kitsch. Taken up by architects themselves, they became emblems of wit and irony, and a critique of the consumer society.

Although art-world writers tended to depict everyone outside their circle as victims of the marketing techniques of the capitalist system (as they had done in the nineteenth century), other social critics once again drew a distinction between the responses of the middle and lower classes. In this revised analysis, the middle class continued to relish the products it bought, while the lower class, now differentiated as underprivileged groups, supposedly learned to resort to subversive tactics so that they could exploit the system while undermining it.[81] This view coincided with the art world's image of itself as being outside the society it moralized upon. However, it overlooked certain realities. The aim of most disaffected groups has been not to overthrow the system but to procure a share of its benefits. The measure of the attraction of the middle class is that people actively sought to join it in order to improve their lives and the prospects of their children.

Moreover, most participants in the art world, especially architects, are already part of the social establishment and belong to well-defined institutions within it. It is, therefore, disingenuous to present themselves as society's conscience when even artists and critics use the resources and methods of the marketplace, which also pays for, distributes, and endorses their work. Clearly, most people nowadays are willing participants in the dominant socioeconomic system. By condemning the middle class for yielding to it, art-world writers have attempted to gain a paradoxical success. They have denied their own complicity in that system, while protecting the power it gives them.

If art-world activists restricted themselves to producing and distributing works for the benefit of their admirers, they would make a significant contribution to the sum of human experience. Unfortunately, they also feel compelled to impose their will on the world at large, and to belittle all other attempts to address the aspirations of ordinary life. They fail to see that the rise of individualistic societies (now more classless than middle class) has rendered this patronizing attitude obsolete. There is no justification in equating a sensible, moderate, progressive existence with a lack of spiritual depth. Nor is there any sanction for claiming that ordinary people lack the need or ability, or even right, to create or adopt their own expressive symbols, so that they may reinforce and enrich the values that sustain them.

Confined to art-world circles, this arrogant standpoint could be taken for what it is: the offensive action of a zealous group attempting to defend its own legitimacy. Applied to buildings, it not only shows a complete misunderstanding of the social role of architecture and its importance to the community as a whole. It also undermines and demoralizes architects themselves, who share many characteristics of the very people their mentors teach them to despise.

4.1 The belief that some societies are naturally superior to others originated in antiquity. It was a self-evident truth for aesthetes who looked back to a golden age for their justification. In *The School of Athens* by Raphael, the assembly clusters around Plato and Aristotle, Pythagoras and Euclid.

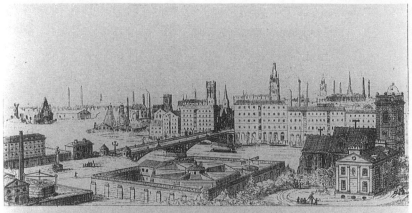

THE SAME TOWN IN 1840

1. St Michael's Tower rebuilt in 1750. 2. New Parsonage House & Pleasure Grounds. 3. The New Jail. 4. Gas Works. 5. Lunatic Asylum. 6. Iron Works & Ruins of St Maries Abbey. 7. St Evans Chapel. 8. Baptist Chapel. 9. Unitarian Chapel. 10. New Church. 11. New Town Hall & Concert Room. 12. Wesleyan Centenary Chapel. 13. New Christian Society. 14. Quakers Meeting. 15. Socialist Hall of Science.

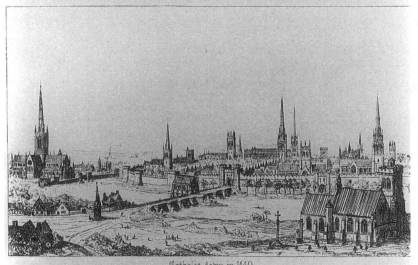

Catholic town in 1440.

1. St Michaels on the Hill. 2. Queens Cross. 3. St Thomas's Chapel. 4. St Maries Abbey. 5. All Saints. 6. St Johns. 7. St Peters. 8. St Alkmunds. 9. St Maries. 10. St Edmunds. 11. Grey Friars. 12. St Cuthberts. 13. Guild hall. 14. Trinity. 15. St Olaves. 16. St Botolphs.

4.2 Once the idea was accepted that the quality of a society is mirrored in its culture, the argument could be made that bad societies produce bad architecture. This was the powerful message of A.W.N. Pugin's comparison between the uplifting spires of a medieval town in 1440 and its prisonlike buildings after the Industrial Revolution in 1840.

4.3 For the cultivated élite, the nineteenth century was bad because of the increasing influence of the new middle class, represented by the French king, Louis Philippe, in this cartoon by Honoré Daumier. Its writers and artists denounced the materialism of their age and asserted their own role as ideologues and taste-makers for society at large.

4.4 The Great Exhibition of 1851, held in the Crystal Palace, was a landmark in this encounter between the middle class and its critics. The household articles displayed by British manufacturers stressed ingenuity, ornamentation, imagery, and allegory.

4.5 Such 'bourgeois' values were dismissed by 'connoisseurs' who advocated a more 'refined' style based on moral strictures that they could categorize as 'aesthetic laws.' This bedstead was designed by the painter Ford Madox Brown and made by William Morris' company in the 1860s.

THE SIX-MARK TEA-POT.

Æsthetic Bridegroom. "IT IS QUITE CONSUMMATE, IS IT NOT?"
Intense Bride. "IT IS, INDEED! OH, ALGERNON, LET US LIVE UP TO IT!"

4.6 Confronted by the growth of democratic societies, nineteenth-century aesthetes reacted in different ways. The 'art for art's sake' advocates retreated into their own circle, which was satirized in *Punch*.

4.7 Others used their authority in an attempt to convert the children of the new industrial classes to their own way of thinking, by teaching them to discover the 'true principles' of design.

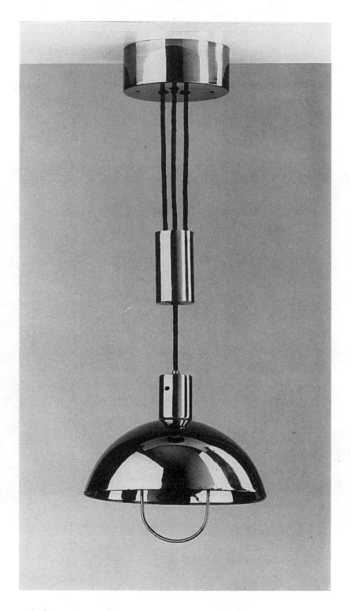

4.8 Some manufacturers were persuaded to try to change the public's taste by mass-producing articles in an approved style. The ceiling lamp designed by Marianne Brandt and Hans Przyrembel at the Bauhaus during the 1920s was made by a Berlin firm.

4.9 Architects took up the same theme that it was their duty to give society the benefit of their professional taste. Depicted as the victim of the middle class, the working class was viewed as the natural recipient of a stripped-down style that architects themselves had come to admire. The Dammerstock estate in Karlsruhe, Germany, built in 1929, was designed by Walter Gropius and Otto Haesler.

4.10 With enough money to buy what they like on the open market, middle-class families have largely resisted this professional attempt to shape their home surroundings.

4.11 Shelf ornaments (sculpture) in a middle-class home.

4.12 Architects denounced this affront to their authority and imposed their own vision on large areas of our cities. When this was judged a failure, they simply blamed it on their materialistic clients. Park Avenue, New York.

4.13 The most invasive intervention by architects in recent decades has been in the new towns that they have been empowered to design. In Cumbernauld, Scotland, for example, the whole central area for a population that has now reached 50,000 was envisaged as a single megastructure under the architects' control.

4.14 The majority of people still have little say in the design of their own towns. Their main success through the conservation movement has been to limit the harm that most architects do. Even old reused industrial sheds like those renovated by Norman Hotson on Granville Island, Vancouver, have come to be preferable to architects' architecture.

5 Class and Architects

*Architects share the same kind of
social values as the majority of other
people. Only their training isolates
them from the rest of the community.*

The division that exists between architects and the community at
large is obviously not inevitable. This would only follow if art (or
more properly, symbols) was something exceptional, that is beyond
the grasp of ordinary people. Unfortunately, this is exactly what
architects are taught to believe.

The proposition that art represents rare intellectual or emotional or
spiritual insights implies that the role of artist calls for very special
human qualities. But this seems to be another case of the art world
defining the larger world in terms of its own claims. Feminist writers
have shown that articles such as quilts were excluded from consideration as art because they did not fit into the art world's mythology.[1]
Aboriginal communities have also provided evidence that art-making
can be a normal activity in which everyone might express their own
aesthetic impulses, or be chosen to participate in traditional ceremonies.[2] How the role of artist became specialized is unknown. Possibly
the individual who seemed most successful in communicating with
the supernatural, or showed the greatest skill in creating the settings
required for its evocation, came to be treated with extra respect by
the rest of the group. Or it may have seemed easier to control supernatural forces through a limited number of agents. Whatever the
reason, it was probably the perceived discrepancy between the com-
monplaceness of most artists as human beings, and the power of
their work to affect their admirers, that first led to the idea of the
Muse, a goddess who inspired ordinary mortals or used them as her
intermediary. If poets, as Plato suggested, were touched by a divine

madness akin to prophecy, they themselves did not have to be any-thing special.[3] On the contrary, the less sophisticated the better, so that no worldly complications would impede the flow of art. The popular story of Giotto illustrated the legend; the ignorant shepherd boy discovered by Cimabue, drawing sheep on a rock with a pointed stone.[4]

Where this stereotype did not seem convincing, the Renaissance contributed another: the boastful, lustful, brawling, but immensely talented artist like Benvenuto Cellini, hustling his way through the sixteenth century.[5] This idea of the artist living life to the full (and thereby being better prepared than ordinary people to depict its essential qualities) resurfaced in the nineteenth century. Among those later to be credited with genius, Toulouse-Lautrec wallowed in vice, Gauguin sought revelation in the South Seas, and van Gogh was reduced to self-mutilation and suicide. A few generations later, another group of alienated artists, called the beat generation, took to the road, seeking spiritual illumination through drugs, religion, and sex.[6]

But while other artists might assume they possess exceptional qualities, architects do not readily fit this description. One research study in the 1950s that attempted to characterize the personality traits of a group of American architects who were judged talented by their colleagues, concluded that they were especially sensitive and intu-itive, and had wide-ranging interests – including some that were at the time considered feminine. They were also highly motivated and conceited. On the other hand, the study showed that architects, unlike writers, did not externalize their inner states of being, nor did they, unlike scientists, stress intellectual thought.[7]

Historical examples would go even farther. Charles Barry led a simple domestic life, ruminating over his designs within the family circle. Charles Follen McKim was urbane and reserved. It was said that Richard Norman Shaw might have been taken for a successful politician.[8] One may conclude that architects do not have to be excep-tional human beings in a general sense, to be considered especially creative in an architectural sense.

Certainly their training does not encourage the sort of intellectual or emotional – let alone spiritual – exploration of life that is supposed to be embodied in works of art and, specifically, in the designs they produce. In France, architectural practice was explicitly codified and controlled by the ruling establishment. In Britain, its forms were handed down from one generation of architects to another by the pupilage system of apprenticeship in offices. This institutionalization of architecture as a profession rather than as an art was further advanced in the United States, when a few influential architects decided to rescue architecture from its practice as a trade or business, by emulating the French ideal.

The first professional program in the United States opened at the Massachusetts Institute of Technology in 1868.[9] Students of the École des Beaux-Arts attended lectures at the school, but they learned to design in outside *ateliers* under the patronage of practising architects. The Americans transformed the European method, establishing design studios taught by professors – the first such professor at MIT was the Beaux-Arts trained Frenchman, Eugène Létang – and thereby incorporated architectural education into the general university system. By the mid-twentieth century, there was a worldwide chain of architectural schools. These brought architects firmly into the ranks of the accepted middle class, while entrenching the profession's preoccupation with its own concerns.

Whereas artists might be thought to provide individual insights into the nature of existence, architects have traditionally worked in collective styles based on design conventions. While, historically, these conventions were developed in conjunction with the patron class, the separation of architecture into a service profession has meant that they are now largely formulated within the profession itself. It is these conventions that provide the meaning that architects perceive in the buildings they design. This signification is obtained through the layout of a site, the arrangement of a plan, the composition of forms, or the treatment of detail. Myths are generated concerning their beauty, logic, appropriateness, or relevance; their sense of order, mystery, vitality; their position in the built, natural, or social environment; their relationship to the activities they house and to the institutions they service; their response to the materials and methods they employ; their reaction to the past and their image of the future; and their credibility as the right perceptual mode. All this must be done with rectangles, triangles, and circles; with walls and windows, roofs and staircases; by the disposition of solids and voids; and through the surface finish of materials, and the detailing of building elements.

The purpose of an architect's education has been to pass on and teach the neophyte to manipulate these conventions. Possibly the advocates of a university-type education thought that it would raise architecture to the level of an intellectual discipline. On the contrary, the theory and practice that resulted confirmed that architecture was still to be pursued in terms of styles that did not encourage rational discourse. The replacement of the École des Beaux-Arts by the Bauhaus as an international model in the mid-twentieth century had significant pedagogic and stylistic consequences, but only accentuated the underlying contradictions of an architectural training. The Beaux-Arts system of instruction had been based on the study of principles and precedents. The preliminary course initiated by Johannes Itten at the Bauhaus also looked for underlying aesthetic laws but attempted to confirm these by direct experience as well as through historical example.[10] This search for principles through research appeared to do away with outdated prescriptions. In practice, however, it only re-placed one dogma by another, because the method was tied to stylistic preferences.

In Itten's case – given his stated intention of liberating his students' creative potential, and the prevailing bias towards expressionist art – the images his students produced in their spiritual odyssey did suggest some sort of personal exploration (although even Itten was apt to indulge in emotional outbursts when this took an unwanted turn).[11] His successor, László Moholy-Nagy, who had previously ordered his paintings for an exhibition by telephone, dismissed such elements of subjectivism and mysticism. Moholy-Nagy treated the exercises he set as if they were experiments in a scientific inquiry that would uncover the reciprocal laws of aesthetics and aesthetic experience.[12] That is, his intended aim was not that students would find their own personal (if limited) truth, but that it would be seen to reside in the forms of art and design, and reveal itself through the nature of human biology, which determined its perception and response. At the same time he had no doubt that the visible outcome of these experiments would be in line with the sort of art that had been produced by abstract artists like himself. In other words, his students were given both the underlying theory and the outward forms to match it – in fact, both rules and models, just as in the despised Beaux-Arts. No doubt, Moholy-Nagy's enthusiasm and the novelty of the results that were demanded, did encourage both master and students to feel that they were in the vanguard of an aesthetic discovery. But even Moholy-Nagy warned that the outward forms generated in this search for absolute truth could easily degenerate into a superficial style.[13]

This is just what happened when the schools of architecture, which subsequently based their method of teaching design on the Bauhaus preliminary course, tied their exploratory exercises to the Modern style, where they took on their own justification as proof of its validity. Aesthetic biases that had been largely explicit under the Beaux-Arts system now became concealed and implicit. Instead of being told that the Modern style represented the correct image of mid-twentieth-century architecture, and having its principles and forms explained to them, students had to acquire this understanding through a series of exercises whose goals were largely prejudged but unstated.

The fall of the Modern style changed the outward result but left the method intact. Students are still required to find their way through a series of exercises that invite rational thought while subverting it by the stylistic demands of the day. This result is achieved through a sort of Socratic dialectic reinforced by a system of punishments and rewards. These emerge mainly through the verbal exchanges that occur at individual or open critiques. There, students are required to defend their designs within the context of the pretentious (and often groundless) claims of current fads. Normally utilizing a superficial knowledge of other disciplines, laden with the clichés of the day, and essentially motivated by unstated aesthetic preferences, the exchange determines the relative merits of the projects according to their meaningfulness for the jury of architects present.[14] For students who would like to resist this affront to common sense, and learn to design buildings rather than follow the latest architectural movement, there is always the need to pass the course (and later to obtain the necessary licence to practise).[15]

This system of moulding professional opinion by covert persua-
sion, sustained over the four to six years that architectural programs
typically last and with design instruction occupying from one-third
to two-thirds of the scheduled time, guarantees a large measure of
conformity to the prevailing style – usually presented in the guise of
the significant, or only, issues of the day.

Parenthetically, it should be noted that this disposition to follow
fashion is so much part of the *modus operandi* of the profession that
it includes architects no matter where they live. Specialists from, or
trained in, the West who initially set up schools of architecture
abroad did not simply transplant a pedagogic system but also ex-
ported the mental outlook that engendered it. In India, for example,
students have not only been required to study their own architectural
history but also that of the West, complete with its roster of cult
figures.[16]

Furthermore, the same architectural heroes that occupy the minds
of Western students are promoted through publications that serve the
profession globally. Within a dozen years of Robert Venturi producing his first influential design, his images were spread across the
world through architectural magazines, and his ideas translated into
Japanese as well as all the major European languages. Similarly, more
belatedly but even more spectacularly, Venturi's contemporary, Frank
Gehry, became an instant media celebrity in the late 1970s when he
remodelled his home using corrugated metal, chain-link fencing, and
angled shapes.

The particular subjects that make up an architectural education in
schools in different countries vary considerably in detail. But because
of the emphasis on design, courses are usually oriented towards the
knowledge required to support design, and made subordinate to it.
In this situation, even a technical subject like building construction
can be seen to be closely related to the prevailing tastes of the design
studios. While it might seem odd to talk about a Neo-Gothic or Post-
Modern engineer, architects are often characterized in this manner.
For architects, a technique is only relevant when it enables them to
construct what they design. When there is a change in stylistic preferences, some parts of the existing building technology also become
outdated, not because of any functional shortcomings, but because of

their appearance. In the past fifty years, for instance, facades have been conceived in terms of masonry, masonry and metal, poured concrete, metal and glass, precast concrete, and once again masonry, at a rate of change that has inhibited the rational solution of basic functional problems.

Consequently, although the material production of building forces a degree of conformity from below, it is the architectural ideology that provides the overriding direction from above. And it is this view of architecture that is supported by the history of architecture courses that provide the major theoretical underpinning for the practice of design. As we have seen, instead of encouraging the investigation of the general evolution of buildings as social artefacts, this type of history highlights the designated artworks of particular individuals or groups and attempts to organize them into an orderly chronology of styles. The projection of this system into the contemporary scene supports and extends the belief that architecture stems from a few gifted individuals who create the most meaningful architecture for their time. These are the models that are cited in the design studio. And these (and their advocates) supply the images and rationalizations that provide the framework for the practice and criticism of design.

In this context, design owes little to any exploration of the outer world or even the inner self. Rather, it focuses on learning how to manipulate – or, more rarely, add to – the current set of stylistic conventions. This activity inhibits the dispassionate search for knowledge or understanding normally associated with a university education. Instead, dogma favours credulity over intelligent inquiry. Borrowing ideas from other disciplines that have been only superficially understood and inappropriately applied, architectural credos often include assertive propositions that do not encourage reasoned analysis. Being restrictive in their scope and frequently intolerant, they rely on faith and a suspension of disbelief rather than logic.

This leads to the sort of narrow-mindedness that permeates architectural thought. If 'modernism' is out and 'historicism' is the order of the day (as in the Classical dress of the housing blocks by Ricardo Bofill outside Paris, or the Neo-Gothic image of the glass-sheathed towers in Pittsburgh by Johnson and Burgee), then it is no use point-

ing out that the professional appeal of a style like Art Nouveau for
architects – who were probably no better nor worse than their suc-
cessors – was precisely that it looked like a new art; and that, far
from being totally rejected by the general public, its offshoot, Art
Deco or the Moderne (as it was called to distance it from the 'real'
Modern style), was used as a symbol of sophisticated living in popular movies of the period such as *Grand Hotel*.[17]

The doctrine of Neo-Rationalism provides another example.[18] In its
story line, 'typology' was supposed to be the generating principle of
'form,' which is received through the 'collective memory' and embodied in 'the city.' The authorized prototype was the triangular-
roofed rectangular form of the romanticized Classical primitive hut,
and it was considered heresy to suggest that the enormous proliferation of buildings in recent centuries demonstrates that even a roof
can come in many shapes – flat, shed, hipped, gambrel, mansard,
pyramidal, domical, conical, curved, parabolic, catenary – to say
nothing of the exotic roofscapes of the Château de Chambord or S.
Basil's Cathedral in Moscow.

While such philosophizing affects to delve deep into the condition
and meaning of existence, it all takes place in the art world itself,
where it spins its own self-satisfying fictions. Even the recent flirta-
tion with 'deconstructivism,' which claimed to question architectural
assumptions, treated the subject as an amusing critique of art world
manners. Acute angles, clashing forms, and varied materials spoke
to their admirers of penetrating insights into the conventions of their
predecessors. Missing was any serious attempt to understand the
motivations of the architectural profession and the underlying causes
of its past and present practices. The dominion of 'art' remained un-
touched, not even recognized as an issue, and the fundamental questions concerning the role of building in society were once again
evaded.

It is here that ideology has been confused with theory. If theory is
defined as a systematic explanation of a subject based on a set of
general propositions, then architecture as it has evolved has been
virtually incapable of achieving this goal. When the Classical tradition was believed to represent the only ideal architecture, some
semblance of a general theory was realizable by simply describing its

forms and rules. Once it became apparent that there were other styles that were equally acceptable yet different, it was also clear that Classical 'theory' could not be used to stand for architecture as a whole. While some later writers attempted to find underlying principles that would be applicable to any stylistic type, most followed the Classical example and looked for justifications of their own tastes.[19] The result has been that any consistent attempt to construct a theory of architecture has been replaced by a series of self-serving rationalizations centred around specific styles.

How and why particular styles come and go is still largely uncharted – although the fate of Lever House provides an example of this process. Certainly the art-world press constitutes an entire industry in itself, replete with journalists, critics, and historians, devoted to deciding reputations and establishing their significance. It is in this push and pull of words and images that connections are made, ideas put forward, theories approved, principles affirmed, myths created, meanings attributed, preferred forms endorsed, details settled, terminology agreed upon, dissenters denounced, supporting examples praised, and aesthetic norms confirmed. And it is this version of events that emerges as the current state of the art to be handed down to the profession as the authorized standard of informed taste.

Characteristically, all such styles and their attendant theories are presented as if they had an objective reality of their own – that they arose from deep underlying conditions where some basic purpose, thrust, characteristic, or quality of design determined its own realization; that this emerged from a building's form or function or meaning, or was derived from its geometry or construction or type, or that it stemmed from nature or society or history or the city, or some other abstract entity; in short, that the favoured style was not invented as an aesthetic response to the act of making symbols out of buildings, but pre-existed it; and that, at bottom, architectural styles create themselves (although the term 'style' itself is frowned upon because it suggests its own vulnerability).

This has been the architectural realm. And most architects have been followers within it. For the majority of architects do not attempt to create their own symbolic language but adapt one or, more usually, aspects or pieces of a few, that are currently in vogue. Their own scope of invention is limited to the manipulation of these selected conventions. The layout of plans – how they should be arranged; the treatment of structure – to expose or conceal it; the selection of materials – concrete or brick finish, for example; the treatment of forms – to be viewed as abstract shapes or as building elements like doors and roofs; the attitude towards decoration – to use or not to use it; the allusion to historical motifs – prohibited or permissible: it is within the context of such received conventions that stylistic choices are made on a daily basis. This is the design material that architects work with. And they are taught to believe that it embodies profound truths which they are destined to reveal.

It has been suggested that the motivation of this stance lies in the rewards architects have striven for over centuries: money, status, and power.[20] However, there is no evidence that the use of metaphysics as a device to achieve these goals actually promotes their attainment. For example, statistics show that the architects' attempt to distance themselves from engineers by wrapping themselves in philosophical speculation has had no financial reward. The connection might even be adverse, considering that visual artists, their closest associates in the art world, have a low value in monetary terms. In the latest Canadian statistics, architects generally earned roughly the same as civil engineers. Visual artists earned less than half that amount.[21] Evidently, metaphysics is not necessarily a prized commodity.

Status is more difficult to measure and has to be considered at two levels: those of the profession and of the individual architect. Sociologists have investigated the concept of occupational prestige since the 1920s. While there is continuing debate over its definition, their research does give some indication of the way different types of work are commonly viewed. Once again, using this measure, there is little difference to be noted between architects and civil engineers, both of whom belong to respected professions.[22] Architects, of course, do not see it this way. Trained to hero-worship, they tend to bask in the reflected glory of their idols, and dream that someday they too may achieve the same degree of fame. Yet even this promise of prestige is more fictitious than real. Wright received exceptional publicity for an architect, but was still probably less famous than the actor, Gary Cooper, who portrayed his romanticized persona in the film *The Fountainhead*.[23]

The third reward, power, seems to be the actual inducement that motivates architects – not general power in a political or economic sense, but the power to impose their opinions on others. Clearly, architects have little of the political influence that in North America is largely the province of lawyers. Two-thirds of Canada's prime ministers have been lawyers. In the United States, lawyers have been termed the 'high priests of politics.'[24] In comparison, American architects were found to have few opportunities to make important government decisions.[25]

Lawyers, also, have considerable influence in the business world according to American and British studies of outside directors on company boards. In the British study, they constituted 25 per cent of the total.[26] In the American study, they made up 12 per cent, whereas a group connected to construction, engineering, and architectural services, which probably included both architects and engineers, accounted for only 1.5 per cent.[27]

The power that architects seek, then, is not outside their occupation but in the field of building design itself; that is, in their capacity to dictate the physical surroundings in which large numbers of people are required to live. An examination of one of the British new towns suggests how this has been achieved.

Having, in 1956, decided to build the new town of Cumbernauld in Scotland, the government set up a corporation board, which in turn looked for professional advice to help it prepare a master plan. In this case, it chose Hugh Wilson, who was a not unusual product of his day.[28] Wilson had trained at an ordinary school of architecture, apprenticed in an ordinary architect's office, and, not being in the military during World War II, had become the city architect for Canterbury by the end of it. A few years later he had assumed a second title of planning officer, and it was as Chief Architect and Planning Officer that he received his job at Cumbernauld.

One might think that as an employee of the corporation board, Wilson would have been expected to reflect the social values the board had agreed should structure the resettlement of seventy thou-

sand fellow citizens. On the contrary, Wilson brought his own ideas
on social life – for other people – with him. Up till then, new towns
had been organized into neighbourhood units. Wilson rejected this
idea and declared that Cumbernauld should be more compact with
a higher population density and less open space.[29] The town was
therefore planned as a single unit, with a multi-level centre on the
ridge of a hill containing all the main shops and civic and cultural
facilities.

That Wilson was in no way more, and was perhaps less, qualified
to make social judgments than anyone else is apparent from his
previous career. Certainly, architects tend to distance themselves
from the ordinary world by their narrow focus on their own professional values. Wilson's employers, however, did not distinguish
between his professional knowledge and his social judgments. Having hired a specialist, they were disposed to take his advice. His
social philosophy came free with the planning of roads and the
layout of houses. They were so merged that it was difficult to see
that a way of life was implicit in what appeared to be practical or
even aesthetic recommendations. Instead of the town's underlying
social philosophy being determined by the people themselves, or by
their representatives, their professional employee provided it under
the guise of his expertise.

But architectural styles or ideologies or fashions are human con-
structs. They are neither value-free nor neutral in content. They stem
from the values of their advocates, who are the international leaders
of the architectural set. If these values were widely shared, the result
would be beneficial to the communities that acquired them with their
buildings. But where they are antagonistic to the public interest, they
are a barrier to its involvement.

In adopting the styles of their leaders as the basis of their everyday
practice, architects evade their social responsibilities by assuming that
styles are merely aesthetic in content. They also produce the gap
between what their heroes proclaim and the public receives. For
architects generally have been unable to break out of their inculcated
bondage to a metaphysical notion that is beyond their grasp. They
cannot abandon their aesthetic pretensions. Their work has to make
reference to some preferred style. And because they have no mastery

– or, often, even comprehension – of the idiom they feel impelled to use, their more practical achievements are largely overlooked.

In this system, architects are judged negatively instead of positively, by how far they fall short of the metaphysical ideal, rather than how well they meet the practical problems they are required to solve.[30] It is this way of thinking that drives critics to focus on the works of a handful of architects, and to disregard totally the collective efforts of tens of thousands of others. Where these conditions exist, where they are scorned by critics, ignored by the public, ruled by the interests and restrictions of their clients, and, most of all, apologetic about their own accomplishments, architects are driven to blame their circumstances for the quality of their designs.

For these everyday practitioners, style is not an overriding conceptual structure through which practical solutions take on form and meaning, but only vague generalizations of the sort of thing that architects do. What they offer their clients and public is not some insightful or transcendental experience achieved through the art of building, but the architects' conventions of their trade, the insignia of art, filtered down through the ranks of the profession, from the works and words of their trend-setting colleagues above.

Confronted by the real world of constraints that tend to limit the shape of building solutions – planning norms, standardized structural systems and components, by-laws, costs, practical requirements, client preferences – there would always be considerable difficulty in transferring an art style from the studio to the streets – a major reason why this so seldom takes place. But instead of ignoring this call to some higher purpose, and finding satisfaction in the ordinary building tasks they are asked to deal with, most architects try to incorporate it into their designs, attempting a copy (though more often a travesty) of its outward imagery. This is the practice, even though many architects themselves dislike the result. It is this version of architecture that the unknowing public receives: a garbled and essentially meaningless simulation of styles that hold deep significance for a very small group of aesthetic specialists who, to complete the irony of the situation, despise their imitators.

Here the art-world system runs up against social realities. Western society has minimized this confrontation by institutionalizing the art world. Artworks are usually located in special buildings that must be visited intentionally if an aesthetic experience is desired: galleries, museums, theatres, concert halls, opera houses. Even books must be read and radio and television turned on. Everyone can choose what they wish to experience. In this respect, architecture is fundamentally different from the other arts. Based on social artefacts, it exists in the public domain, and forms part of our everyday existence. A style like conceptual art might be incorporated into the international art-world canon, but its impact is peripheral, confined to a small group of admirers who must enter specially sanitized (and closely guarded) rooms to see it. Buildings are often huge and always present. When architects use their lingua franca, we get Gothic Revival campuses, Neoclassical city halls, Modern office towers, and Post-Modern housing developments – a random miscellany of aesthetic gleanings from around the world in which ordinary people must live and work and find some meaning and relevance to who and what they are, and wish to be.

This is the 'art' that the profession passes on to the public regardless of whether it wants it or not. Admittedly there have been some general predispositions towards some architectural styles. Children taught Latin might be expected to have some feeling for the Neoclassical architecture advocated by its disciples. Readers of Gothic romances might welcome the enthusiasts of the Neo-Gothic style. But this is only in the very broadest terms. Most people probably do not know the difference between a column or a pilaster, or between decorated and perpendicular, let alone understand the arcane arguments underlying the assertions about why and how they ought to be employed. Conversely, it is difficult to know what the general public brought to Modern architecture, except perhaps the inhibitions of wartime austerity. Nor is it likely that the present-day public has any greater appreciation of the Post-Modern styles that architects currently use.

Because most of the other 'arts' have to be subsidized, usually with public funds, and access to them is controlled, it has become a routine and relatively easy matter to determine who their 'consumers' are. Studies show that only a minority of people are involved in art activities, and that they are more educated and have a higher income and occupational status than the general population.[31] In other words, art is a manifestation of class (although gender affects the particular art form that is favoured).[32] Given the information usually collected, and the social prestige surrounding art-world activities, the statistics are difficult to interpret. But the size and frequency of the attendance at art galleries, which exhibit the sort of objects that are closest in intent to the designs that architects admire, suggest that only a minority of even this class within the community is involved on a regular basis, notwithstanding the amount of publicity that art receives.[33]

Considered as part of the art world, architecture probably attracts an even smaller segment because it is less publicized and less familiar. Its output comes from a very small, relatively affluent profession, which in North America and Britain comprises less than 0.1 per cent of the population.[34] Moreover, news of architectural products is just as likely to appear on the business pages of the press as among its art reviews, and only a very few buildings are treated as art material. Architecture has only recently begun to receive the same media attention as the other arts, due to a changing set of circumstances.[35] For their part, the new leaders of the profession dropped the professional posture of their predecessors and re-entered the art-world arena, producing designs with more variety and visual appeal. On its side, the publishing industry realized the marketing potential of architecture as another form of art culture, and responded to a growing public interest that was stimulated by the conservation movement.

Architecture has not usually been part of an educational program – at least, not past the kindergarten stage of play with constructional toys. After more than a century of art education in schools, teaching children architecture is still at the experimental stage. In Britain, for example, it has only recently been included in the recommendations for the study of art in a national curriculum.[36] Consequently, it is still common for even university students to be unfamiliar with the names of architects admired by the profession, let alone the buildings they have designed or the theories they stand for. The line of involvement from art through style therefore comes to a virtual halt when it hits the public domain. All the public can respond to is whether buildings are attractive or not.

The standard response of the profession to this widespread ignorance of the design conventions it uses, and the world-view they are intended to convey, is to propose more or better instruction in architectural topics; that is, the same demand that art-world 'experts' have made perennially. This is unlikely to be any more successful than the traditional teaching of literature or art. The problem in this strategy to make the art world's products more acceptable, is located in the nature of the art world itself. This has become more apparent with the increasing level of public education. When only a fraction of the population went beyond the three R's, it could easily be assumed that more education would provide a solution to the lack of awareness of the 'better things in life.'

The rise of the middle class undermined this reasoning. Today, when the amount of schooling that architects receive is no greater than that for other careers in areas like science, engineering, business, or health care, and when the growth of service industries requires a university-trained work force, it has become obvious that education in itself does not necessarily develop a liking for the established art forms. It turns out that the old idea of 'cultivation' was not a by-product of an education, but part of its specific content. In other words, would-be 'cultivated' people must be taught the same conventions that artists have been trained to use.

To achieve this end, 'education' has to be focused specifically on the various modes of artistic expression and their prevailing norms. Not only do these vary but they themselves affect educational theories. The mid-nineteenth-century pedagogical stress on knowledge through imitation derived from academic art; its rejection and replacement in the mid-twentieth century by self-expression reflected the impact of Modern art.

Nor does the acceptance of the conventions of one art form necessarily lead to an appreciation of all or any of the others. There is no direct correlation, for example, between the appreciation of even dance and music. Cultivation, in such a general sense, is not an abstract quality, but the adoption of specific art-world values and practices. In this respect, the argument for teaching people to appreciate art-world products is circular and closed: art is worth teaching because it is art. Those who are unconvinced or indifferent to its claims are simply left outside the system to find their own symbolic fare.

In an odd way, this double standard is paralleled in the manner that governments support the arts. In Canada, for example, it has been government policy since the 1950s to subsidize the arts as an index of the nation's cultural maturity – and, more particularly, though questionably, as a means of evolving and protecting its separate identity. It is also well-known that a small, affluent minority benefits most from this extra financial support. Consequently, in North America at least, there is little attempt to convince the social majority to accept this standard as its own nor, conversely, is there any widespread sense of inferiority at not being able to reach it. In turn, this tolerant attitude reinforces the prevailing sense of individuality and equality, and further isolates the art world as a separate entity.

That the art world's promotion of its own products should have been resisted by a majority of the population is understandable. The symbols the art world has created to support its own interests have evidently lacked the qualities that would provide a similar sense of purpose, meaning, or even pleasure to most people outside it. Conversely, its disdain for other people's concerns only adds to this division. The problem is not that art-world conventions are more difficult to grasp than those of any other group, but that they are essentially irrelevant outside their own circle.

This should not come as a surprise to architects. There is no evidence to indicate that architects have any more liking for the other arts than anyone else. This is particularly true concerning contemporary works. It should therefore require little imagination for them to realize that living among the buildings they design could be like being forced to listen continuously to meaningless sounds, or to walk every day through galleries of meaningless images.

Architects find this difficult to realize because of two aspects of their background. In general, they share the outlook of the socio-economic class to which they belong. But in matters concerning architecture alone, their training in the professional styles of the day ensures that they have more in common with other architects from around the world than with non-architects in their own community.

Unable to impose its views on the public through education, the profession has attempted to protect its jurisdiction by reinforcing and extending it. But neither of these strategies is likely to succeed further in communities where people are becoming more concerned and responsible for their own development, and capable of controlling it. To extricate themselves from the situation they have created, architects would do better to abandon their illusions of authority, and recognize that symbols are human inventions. Rather than seeking a solution in their own practices, they should see that it lies in designing buildings that have wide appeal and derive from a consensus of cooperation.

Inhibited by their long-standing belief that architecture is based on some sort of metaphysical ideal, architects have come to confuse fiction with reality, forgetting that it is they themselves who helped create the myth. In consequence they are ill-prepared to look for architectural solutions that satisfy the community as a whole. Yet here is where the challenge lies: to help reveal the aspirations of the people around them, and to embody them in the structure of their towns.

The problem is how to discover what people want. As it has evolved, the art-world tradition has fluctuated between two positions: that art has its own intrinsic qualities that are outside human jurisdiction, and that art deals with such profound matters that it is outside ordinary human comprehension. This has led to people being divided into 'us' and 'them': the enlightened, who respond to art, and everyone else, who does not. The concept of 'popular culture' that comes from this attitude has been ensconced in academic circles by the Library of Congress, which still differentiates between works 'produced for a mass audience' under this heading, and 'the arts,' which it includes under 'intellectual life.'[37]

The same antithesis sparked the fascination with pop art, which gained notoriety by using 'lowbrow' images to create 'highbrow' art. In architecture these extremes were represented by the work of the 'masters' of the day, and by typical subdivision housing. Analysing the design characteristics of market-oriented building types (as opposed to employer-directed styles, which architects rationalize as objectively valid and without mercenary intent), architects tried to expose – and bridge – the differences between professional and non-professional taste.

Other theorists have argued that people cannot be treated as an undifferentiated mass. Writing from a sociological standpoint in the 1960s, Herbert J. Gans attempted to outline a more complex taxonomy of taste in which there were five main groups related to standard class divisions, especially levels of education.[38] Although he noted that it was common for both producers and consumers of cultural items to cross these boundaries, and for tastes to change, Gans also sought to define the specific characteristics of each group. The 'lower middle culture,' which he posited as the dominant taste of the post–World War II period, bought Degas prints, watched sitcoms on television, read *Reader's Digest*, enjoyed musicals, and presumably provided the residents of the burgeoning suburbs that architectural critics wrote about.

Recent research on popular culture has introduced further modifying factors of gender, race, ethnicity, and the like, but what effect these have on architectural judgments is still largely unexplored except at a practical level, such as the advantages gained by special facilities for the elderly and disabled. Nor have such caveats diminished the success of the counter-claim that people generally have essentially similar tastes. Instead, this assumption has gained new legitimacy as a result of the conservation movement.

Predating the current concern for old buildings, an interest in primitive dwellings had been stimulated in architectural schools by László Moholy-Nagy, who had set up a 'New Bauhaus' in Chicago in 1937 – subsequently the Institute of Design. As part of their basic course, students were required to design their own primitive house, the idea being that through this exercise they would rediscover the functional principles underlying architectural form.[39] This interest was broadened by Sibyl Moholy-Nagy to include vernacular buildings, which were the subject of her book *Native Genius in Anonymous Architecture in North America*, published in 1957.[40] Here again, the motivation was to uncover fundamental truths about architectural design, but now the lessons expected to be learned went far beyond functional considerations. The study of such buildings was intended to reveal the source of not only their aesthetic merit, but also their spiritual content and social import.

Later writers have advanced variations on this theme. At one end of the range is the simple assertion that there are 'common sense' rules to be gleaned from the past, such as that buildings should be in scale, or that they should incorporate local materials.[41] At the other extreme, the alleged virtues of vernacular architecture have inspired (in an update of William Morris) a sweeping critique of post-industrial society. It condemns virtually everything that has been planned or built in the past few hundred years, and proposes returning to a more 'civilized' existence through the reintroduction of traditional forms (often using expedients that seem to exploit the methods and benefits of an advanced capitalist economy while rejecting its ideology). Exemplifying this search for a universal prescription, and the obsession of its purpose, Christopher Alexander, in the matter of a decade, went from enumerating an ostensibly empirical 'pattern language' of design deduced from our 'timeless way of building,' to pledging to divulge the secret rule that underlies all human construction.[42]

This endeavour is no different from the time-honoured art-world practice of attempting to abstract universal and timeless principles from the canon of its work, except the argument is turned upside-down, so that the buildings that are supposed to embody eternal truths are those outside the art-world canon. Society is still divided into 'us' and 'them,' but in this scenario the repository of architectural virtues is not elitist 'art' but 'popular culture' – only not that of the present day, but of a bygone era when the ordinary people who made and bought it were somehow immune to the degrading effects of commercialism.

Undoubtedly, the study of buildings of any kind, whether 'artistic,' 'vernacular,' or 'popular,' is a beneficial pursuit, which can provide insights about individual and social characteristics of taste that are both enlightening and enriching. But just as art-world theorists have failed to uncover a fixed set of immutable laws, there is no reason to expect that scrutinizing other sets of buildings will be any more rewarding, for exactly the same reasons.

Merit is not embedded in objects in some metaphysical way, nor are human beings biologically programmed to respond to it. There is no deep structural accord between people and their products, which reflects some cosmic purpose. Symbol-making is an interactive activity that takes place between them, and while products remain constant, people often do not. This is especially true in the Western tradition, where change has become the norm as well as a social ideal. In this context, people are more than the sum of their past.

This applies just as much to the general population as to any group within it such as the specialized world of art. The rate at which the art world has changed its styles has come to be exaggerated by its emphasis on originality and its overt and explicit involvement in aesthetic commerce. Non-specialists tend to rely on longer-lasting traditions and customs. But they, like the art world, are continually offered alternatives by would-be suppliers of both ideological and material products from which they select their symbolic fare. And they are just as likely to change their minds, both individually and collectively.

Paris provides a cautionary lesson on trying to lay down rules based on past experience. Reshaped by Napoleon III and G.E. Haussmann during the mid-nineteenth century, its existing fabric was overlaid with a new network of roads. The old passageways were swept away. Wide boulevards cut through built-up areas. Nothing was allowed to stand in the way of progress. Historic buildings, medieval houses, archaeological remains – all became part of the demolition statistics of the period, which peaked in 1867 when more than two thousand buildings were wholly or partially destroyed. Not even churches were immune; the eleventh-century S. Marine fell with the rest of the Île de la Cité; the choir of S. Leu was sliced off to allow the Boulevard de Sébastopol to pass straight by.[43] The result of all this reconstruction was that Paris came to be regarded by a broad spectrum of people as one of the most beautiful cities in the world.

A century or so later and a similar public consensus has come to support the opposite extreme of preservation. Even obsolete factories and old sheds are now protected from demolition. Yet there is no contradiction between these two events. Advocates like to press their favourite cause in terms of some absolute right and wrong, but experience teaches us that no matter how persuasive a particular doctrine might seem at the moment, it is based on opinions that are open to change. Ultimately, people create values, not the reverse, and people are too complex to fit any deterministic theory.

Nor is the human race a single undifferentiated mass (whether this is portrayed as 'society' or as 'Homo sapiens'). People not only vary among themselves, but also within their own lifetimes. It follows that what is needed is not another set of styles or rules, but a process whereby people collectively can realize their ambitions – in just the same way that the professional class has so successfully fulfilled its own.

Unfortunately, unlike the art world, the real world lacks its own organization. It has no forum where its needs can be debated, and until recently it has had little opportunity to voice even its objections. Relatively few persons are involved as purchasers of buildings, or as the elected or public officials who regulate them. To some extent, the general public has an indirect influence on the design of buildings such as speculative housing and shopping malls, because its custom is essential to their financial success – a factor missing in other building types like offices or hospitals. But, on the whole, it has taken no part in the design of either individual buildings or the overall urban environment they form. Yet this is where the resolution to the split between the real world and the art world is to be found.

The trend towards direct community participation in its own concerns, which originated in the 1950s, first caught public attention with the rise of protest groups operating outside and against institutionalized centres of authority. In a way, this was only another step in the struggle for self-realization that has taken place over the past few centuries. Politically, the impulse contributed to the American and European uprisings against autocratic rule, and later to the liberation movements in countries controlled by European states. Socially, it led to workers confronting their bosses, and to women demanding equality with men. Even in art, it encouraged the belief in personal creativity and the revolt against the dominance of the academies.

For the generation of the 1960s, the civil rights, peace, and environmental movements were part of a widespread attempt by people to gain a direct voice in decisions that affected them. In architecture, this involvement was initiated by the United States government through its housing bills, which offered federal aid to local communities. The 1949 Housing Act made a public hearing mandatory before land could be acquired for slum clearance.[44] The guidelines for implementing the provisions for urban renewal in the 1954 Housing Act required 'citizen participation,' so that everyone would feel committed to the process.[45] More particularly, they directed that a special effort should be made to include 'minority' groups, which marked an important attempt to give the traditionally powerless the opportunity to defend their own interests.

There was considerable sympathy for this move. The impact of the bulldozer method of dispersing slum inhabitants, instead of rehousing them, made urban renewal controversial. Occurring at the same time was the civil rights movement, with its images of 'sit-in' demonstrators and interstate bus 'freedom riders' being brutally attacked by law enforcement officers unleashed by civil authorities who seemed to be out of control. The middle class was normally expected to support the governmental establishment. Now, while well-doers offered their help to the underprivileged (so that, for example, some dedicated architects worked with poor communities), average middle-class citizens realized that they also lacked adequate influence over their own affairs, even though they constituted the social majority. Their response was to circumvent the normal political system, and to take over the methods developed in the civil rights movement to attain their own ends.

A newsworthy example of this type of action occurred in 1961 in New York, when Jane Jacobs organized her Greenwich Village neighbourhood to have its designation as a blighted area rescinded by the city administration.[46] Actually, the bulldozer period of redevelopment, which took place in New York during the 1950s, had just given way to a more sophisticated program of urban conservation and renovation under new direction, and the city officials believed, with some justification, that they were responding to the needs of the community. Jacobs neither trusted their intentions nor accepted their opinions. Assembling a coalition of diverse groups, in less than a year she had forced the city administration to abandon its proposal. Culminating this action was an open meeting of the city planning commission where residents shouted down its chairman, and one of them was carried out feet first by the police.

The ideas that had motivated Jacobs' intervention were also spread by the publication of her book *The Death and Life of Great American Cities*, which was the first sweeping attack on the urban theories of

Le Corbusier, foretelling the architectural profession's own ostensible change of mind.[47] By the end of the decade, the idea that people should have a voice in the design of their own environment had been widely accepted. In Britain, for example, the Town and Country Planning Act of 1968 stipulated that planning authorities should invite representations from interested persons, while the Skeffington Report of the following year expressed the belief that the growing interest in public participation was a valuable development, and explored the means by which it might be practically achieved.[48] Direct citizen involvement had come to be seen as a valid extension of the democratic process.

Without legislative enforcement, architects have shown little inclination to follow this example. Being more protected than planners by their professional mystique and less accountable to elected governments, they have been largely unwilling to expose their work to public debate. Among the exceptions are the few who have attempted to practise participatory design. Ralph Erskine's Byker Housing Estate in Newcastle, England, begun in 1969, has been cited widely as a prototype of this approach.[49] The example also reveals its difficulties. In one respect, Erskine's involvement of the local community was only an extension of the functionalist position that architects should satisfy the needs of their buildings' users. His innovation was to argue that instead of extrapolating those needs from the architect's own life experience (and other outside sources), they should be elicited from the users themselves.

Erskine still thought of (enlightened) architects as 'do-gooders' whose duty was to bestow the benefits of their architectural knowledge on less favoured groups. He also took it for granted that the (competent) architect's position was the correct one, and he was quite prepared to enforce his own ideas – as is evident from the overall design of Byker Estate, which bears more than a passing resemblance to earlier projects by him. Rather than viewing citizen participation as a partnership among equals, he believed that it allowed him as a member of the middle class to gain insight into how other (working-class) people lived.[50]

Other examples, which became well-known because their designs were admired by the architectural world, have had different types of client groups and used different methods. For the medical faculty buildings at Catholic University of Louvain in Belgium, for instance, not only were the students invited by Lucien Kroll to collaborate with his architectural team, but so were the construction workers, who made their own creative contribution to the final project.[51] If these were special client groups, a third example could be viewed as a metaphor for society as a whole, because the people involved were of the same social standing as their architects. In this case, the congregation of S. Matthew's Parish Church in Pacific Palisades, California, employed the firm of Moore, Ruble, Yudell in 1980 to produce a building that would meet with the approval of at least two-thirds of its members. The architects responded by holding group workshops and preparing alternative plans to ensure that a suitable design would result.[52]

How successful these examples of participatory design have been is open to debate. Viewing the problem from the initial American experience with disadvantaged groups, one writer distinguished eight broad types of citizen participation, ranging from 'manipulation' to 'citizen control.'[53] Depending on one's reading of the methods used, Byker Estate could be said to come under the classification of 'tokenism,' where the people were invited to give advice, but the architects and their employers made all the decisions. Two decades later, at the end of the 1980s, advocates of participatory design in Britain – or as it was also called, 'community architecture' – were still unable to point to more than a very few projects that could be said to be under the control of the people affected by them.[54]

The situation is still not essentially different even where 'the people' are of the same socio-economic class as architects and have considerable political leverage. The traditional relationship that continues to operate between the two groups still undermines the process. As long as architects themselves set the agenda for the public's participation, they probably cannot help manipulating the results, whatever their intentions. Organizing meetings, selecting examples, leading discussions, proposing alternatives, providing 'technical' guidance, interpreting reactions, drawing conclusions: architects tend to leave little space for a significant change in the public's role. At this stage, the participatory process is only an interim palliative, the

end of one era rather than the beginning of another. While exposing
the distortions of the traditional relationship between architects and
their community, it deceives people into believing that they are being
invited to share in the power held by a set of altruistic professionals,
when in reality the community itself possesses the actual power to
pursue its own social aims.

The lack of self-confidence shown by the public is understandable
considering its historical situation. The virtual monopoly maintained
by the art world has made it difficult for other people to value their
own judgments. There is no extensive literature to support their
position, few writers to romanticize or theorize about their possessions, no network of museums to legitimate their taste. Being
outside the established system, they are not serviced by the architectural profession, yet they are forced to turn to architects for their
advice and help as they lack any other access to the skills necessary
to realize their own ambitions. The crucial issue, however, is not
whether they have to make use of a profession that, historically, has
ignored their interests, but which of the two participants in this
collaboration will have overall control.

Generally speaking, architects have always had to defer to – or at
least, agree with – the persons who employed them. The romantic
anecdotes about architects who defied popes and princes (as well as
ordinary clients) in defence of their artistic integrity, belong mainly
to the architect's folklore. It is only with regard to the public as a
whole that they have come to believe that their expertise gives them
the right to impose their opinions on it. Paradoxically, this belief has
been fostered by the public's own elected governments, which, having endorsed the professions, tend to accept their advice when it
does not interfere with their own plans.

The rise of direct public intervention has begun to alter this relationship. In urbanized societies, architects work mostly in the public
domain. Even when they are hired and paid by private employers,
the buildings they design utilize the public infrastructure and affect
the public environment. The public therefore has a vital interest in
the overall treatment of individual buildings. From this standpoint,
it is the primary custodian of the buildings that constitute its towns.
In the past, this responsibility has been met by the enactment of

restrictive laws to prevent the worst excesses of private actions. More recently, citizen groups have interceded directly in a negative way, to prevent both private and public developments that they opposed. Acknowledgment of the primacy of the public interest would encourage a more constructive relationship, which would shape the process whereby architectural decisions are made.

Procedures might range from mandatory open reviews of private projects to community control of the design of public buildings. There is much to gain from a situation where public participation is a normal activity rather than a critical response. This shift in outlook has the potential to address many of the problems that have undermined the practice of architecture in the modern world. Architects, who are already accustomed to designing buildings that must satisfy their employers, need only broaden the locus of their design activity. For the public, it allows other different views to be taken into account.

These changes have important consequences. Historically, aesthetic values have come to be shared by architects and their employers from the state, church, and moneyed establishment through the mutual need to validate the symbols that were designed. Similarly, an extended dialogue between architects and the wider community will allow it to become part of the process of endowing buildings with meaning. In this way, people will once again become creators of their own culture rather than merely consumers of it.

As a result, certain academic issues will no longer have any relevance. The debate over whether there is a definable national or regional 'spirit' or character waiting to be 'expressed', with all its attendant metaphysical absurdities and latent bigotry, will be rendered obsolete. Instead of architects trying to establish a sense of identity through self-conscious artful means, it will emerge naturally through the authentic reality of building with the participation of the individuals who constitute the community. Similarly, there is no point in trying to extricate some universal or timeless set of design rules from the previous practices of the (vernacular) past or (commercialized) present, when the choices made by the people themselves will embody their own values and respond to their changing judgments.

Architects have much to gain from this new relationship with their

fellow citizens. They will undoubtedly discover that the new democratic society, which has come into existence while they remained
outside, has many characteristics that they share and endorse. In
addition, participation in the wider community will help to free them
from the demoralizing grip of the art-world system. For, most of all,
if architects are to escape from their self-imposed sense of alienation,
they must change their own perception of themselves and the nature
of their work.

5.1 Artists have often been depicted as the innocent instruments of the muses, like the shepherd who created the first painting by tracing his own shadow.

5.2 Another common assumption is that artists live more intensely than other people, which usually means more sex, drink, and drugs, once associated with bohemian life in Paris.

5.3 Architects generally cannot afford to be so extreme and carefree. They normally operate their firms as businesses, like Burnham and Root, photographed in their nineteenth-century Chicago office.

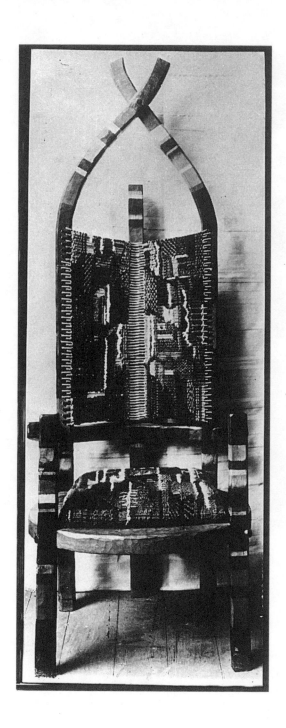

5.4 Their training does not encourage the intellectual, emotional, or spiritual insights they lay claim to. Rather, they are indoctrinated in the current architectural conventions and follow their instructors. An example is provided by two chairs designed by Marcel Breuer while he was a student at the Bauhaus. The first was produced at the end of the Bauhaus' 'expressionist' period in 1921; the second, one year later, at the beginning of its 'constructivist' period.

5.5 Whether students are successful or not in giving 'meaning' to their designs is determined at what are called 'crits,' where their professors require them to engage in esoteric discourse to determine the value of their work.

5.6 For today's architectural specialists, a meaningful experience can even be triggered by odd angles, which represent no less than a fundamental critique of life (an updating of the claim that squares and circles reflected the cosmos).

5.7 Transformed by everyday practice into styles, the connection between forms and their rationalization becomes simpler. A gridded façade is Modern; a stepped façade is Post-Modern.

5.8 Unfortunately, architectural conventions are mostly meaningless to the uninitiated. This should come as no surprise to architects. There is nothing to suggest that they understand the conventions of the other arts any more than anyone else. Art displayed in a world-class museum.

"ROSSI ON THE RISE" — Martin Filler, HOUSE & GARDEN

Herbert Muschamp, VOGUE Emilio Ambasz "Myth Master"

CATHLEEN MCGUIGAN, NEWSWEEK FRANK GEHRY "MAVERICK MASTER"

"Trend-Setting" Robert Stern — Carol Vogel, NEW YORK TIMES

"Why Is Everyone Talking — Carter Wiseman,
About Michael Graves?" SATURDAY REVIEW

Robert Venturi: "Mr. Post-Postmodern"
Douglas Davis,
NEWSWEEK

Paul Goldberger, VOGUE — "Ad-Meier-ing"

"More, More, Moore" — Elizabeth Sverbeyeff Byron,
HOUSE & GARDEN

5.9 'Educating the public' is obviously not the answer. Promoting the latest
celebrity has done little to convince the majority of the population that 'experts'
know which fashion is 'best.'

5.10 This is understandable. Architects used to be part of the ruling
establishment. Nowadays, most people in Western nations want to rule
themselves. Public meetings have become a standard forum for this
exchange of views.

5.11 Architects continue to be more resistant than planners to the idea that they should cooperate with the people who live in and around the buildings they design. One exception has been Lucien Kroll, who encouraged others to participate in the development of the buildings he was responsible for at Catholic University outside Brussels during the 1970s. When people are involved in the design of their own buildings, interest and pleasure are added to their everyday lives.

6 Architects and Design

*If architects would drop their
pretensions, they could help us to
improve the built environment.*

Architects have long asserted that what they do has profound significance: that the buildings they design embody timeless laws, that they parallel nature and the work of God, give order and beauty to an otherwise chaotic and imperfect world, speak for society and mould its behaviour, reflect the human spirit, or give revelational insights into the meaning of life. Bolstering these claims is the overriding assumption that architecture is an autonomous art that deals with transcendental matters, which are outside and above ordinary human activities. In this metaphysical realm, a few geniuses are held to give architectural answers to the foremost questions of the age; in doing so, they attain godlike stature in the eyes of other architects, who find their authority in personalities or styles or even catchwords, and follow them as their spiritual guides.

The architects' conceptual world is therefore shaped like a triangle with the current ideology at its apex, radiating its message downwards. There it is picked up by the second-tier leaders of the profession and the art-world gatekeepers (critics, editors, curators, academics), and propagated and diffused through magazines, books and schools. Adopted by the profession as the style of the day, it is arbitrarily imposed on a defenceless public, by which time the cycle has probably recommenced with another aesthetic manifesto. For its part, the community is left to cope as best it can with the random consequences of this process.

At one level, the consequences are just aesthetic, a matter of imagery that enriches or impoverishes our daily lives. However, architectural ideologies do not confine themselves to aesthetics. They often also incorporate prescriptions for a society's total way of life. For example, in the past century, Neoclassicism was coupled with grandiose vistas climaxed by civic monuments; Arts and Crafts half-timbering with rural idylls; Modern concrete and glass boxes with geometric utopias; Post-Modern historical pastiche with pre-Industrial Revolution shams. The architects who promote these urban forms assume, or lay down, social values without regard for the real people who have to live in them. They believe that their artistic imagination (or genius) gives them the licence to judge how people ought to live, so that issues of social, economic, and political consequence such as the balance of public and private interests, or of free enterprise and government intervention, or of even whether the society is democratic or authoritarian – a system much favoured by architects as long as they are allowed to set the rules – are subordinated to their aesthetic ambitions.

The urban images that architects produce can be taken for what they are: a form of artwork, similarly derived from aesthetic considerations, which may or (usually) may not have any substantive relevance to an actual situation; another type of specialized proposal to set alongside others of a more down-to-earth nature from economists, sociologists, engineers, and the like, when urban decisions are to be made. The threat lies in the legalization of the architectural profession, which enables it to impose its views to a smaller or greater degree as part of the implementation of its services. But even when this abuse of power has been dealt with, the same problem with architects exists in the performance of their real task, which is the design of buildings. For just as with their urban designs, their building designs derive from their own aesthetic interests, which they market with their work as styles. These might sell effectively to a limited clientele, but it is a matter of chance whether they have any relevance for the community as a whole, though it provides the overall means and purpose for their construction.

In contrast, a public- rather than profession-directed process would turn the architect's triangular world-view model upside down. Instead of styles being imposed from above, the enrichment of buildings would take place from below. The generating source would no longer be the single point of the 'genius'-individual's aesthetic doctrine, but the broad base representing the ordinary buildings required by the community. This would provide the common source from which architectural symbolism could accrue. Or, more accurately, it is from this base that another layer of architectural meaning could be added. For, at this primary level, meaning already exists before architectural design occurs. The significance to be found is not in any specific design, but in the disposition and relationship of buildings in general; that is, in what might be called urban planning and urban design, if these terms themselves did not suggest the bureaucratic enforcement of professional concepts.

Much of the information that characterizes the social values of a modern democracy resides in this overall description of its buildings. The type of buildings we erect, their size and facilities, the prominence we give to them, the resources we spend on them, their juxtaposition to one another, their location and accessibility, their degree of openness to public use – these generalized factors that precede and underlie their specific architectural design, or any question of style or art, tell us what sort of community it is. Such terms as 'the wrong side of the tracks,' or 'ghetto,' or even perhaps, as feminist writers have recently argued, 'suburbs,' are usages in our language that indicate whether a society is egalitarian, racist, or sexist.[1]

The different attitudes that distinguish the European street and the North American lot provide a primary illustration of this relationship between urban form and social values. The European street, which stems from Renaissance notions of urbanity, implies a collective order marked by harmony and civility. The North American lot emphasizes individual rights that allow a wide range of social, economic, and design alternatives.

An example of a more specific instance of urban form defining social attitudes is the late-twentieth-century construction of vast interior spaces under private ownership in cities such as Montreal, where whole sections of the downtown area have been enclosed and interconnected. In this case, the people affected have shown themselves willing to give up some of their civil liberties – by allowing themselves to be policed by private security guards who enforce corporate standards of behaviour – in exchange for a well-maintained, climate-controlled environment, free from the typical disadvantages of outdoor city life. Choices such as these give a broad indication of the character of the community that makes them or allows them to occur.

Office towers, apartment buildings, shopping centres, suburban houses – the building blocks of society: these are clear statements about its values. The specific buildings themselves can easily remain mute in this dialogue between a society and its people. Regardless of what architects would like us to believe, most buildings can be viewed (or ignored) simply as ordinary containers of functions, constructed out of the resources at hand, utilitarian structures without overt significance – buildings that go unnoticed because they add nothing explicit to our everyday lives, almost like the city's sidewalks. These are the buildings that can be held to provide the basic material on which architects have traditionally worked.

But even inert buildings do not need the architect's intervention to give them symbolic value. If meaning is implicit in their construction, it can also be achieved through use. As early (or so-called primitive) humans endowed rocks, rivers, or even the wind, with significance, so recent generations have come to find considerable meaning in buildings that were not originally intended to have it. Possibly foreshadowed by writers like Dickens, who anthropomorphized his descriptions of houses, the architect-followers of Morris also came to prefer old houses and barns to the work of other members of their profession.[2] The twentieth century saw the Crystal Palace (designed by a man of affairs) and the Eiffel Tower (designed by an engineer) included among the monuments of art history.[3] In an even more complex interaction between people and buildings, the Manhattan skyline has also been viewed as one of the most evocative images of the modern world, even though it has varied over time in extent, shape, height, detail, and what critics have deemed its architectural quality.[4] This rediscovered ability to endow ordinary buildings with meaning, has allowed conservation groups all over the world to find wide support for retaining old sheds, factories, and warehouses, rather than having them replaced by the new designs of even talented architects. These buildings are not required to have exceptional qualities. Rather they stand as a material record of our past.

In the same way, future generations will know what we were like by looking at our ordinary buildings. For despite what aesthetic specialists like to tell us, life is more profound than art. Experience shows us that we do not need artworks to bring some understanding or purpose or even pleasure to our lives. Utilitarian farm buildings can reflect our geography. The commonplace buildings around us can disclose our history. Standard construction reveals the state of a society's technology. Typical forms give insight into its sense of beauty.

Artworks encode the interests of the art world. Ordinary buildings impartially record all the social conditions that have an impact on them, and bear the imprint of the population as a whole. They represent the basic system of architecture on, and out of, which different groups can form their own particular choices without losing contact with the common values underlying them.

This social basis of architecture is often ignored by architects, who are taught to believe that buildings are primarily a medium for artistic expression. Yet it is this primary level of architecture that provides the groundwork on which people can add their own contribution. What is needed here is design rather than art. Architects have been ambiguous about the word 'design,' using it ambivalently to describe their professional activity of producing architecture, and as a hierarchical term to distinguish architecture from the production of other (less important) artefacts. In the architect's vocabulary, architecture is design raised to the level of art by having been encoded with transcendental meaning; design by itself is only the application of an approved style to products. But regardless of this manoeuvring for occupational status, both represent a professional taste.

Stripped of its metaphysical pretensions and patronizing overtones, design can also be thought of as a normal means of enriching our everyday objects. From this standpoint, buildings can be accepted for the functional containers that they are, and design used to add some extra element of pleasure or interest or symbolism to them. Consequently, most buildings can be left alone because their relevance is implicit rather than intended to be explicit. Nevertheless, there has always been the occasion to enhance buildings to a lesser or greater degree. Various methods have been used to invest build-

ings with other levels of significance and to give them a more dis-
tinctive character. One common way is to make them more visually
pleasing. This might be done by adding decorative features. Or a
building's basic construction may be enhanced through some elabor-
ation of material, form or detail. Another approach is to create a
greater degree of personal engagement between a building and its
viewers through forms and images that evoke emotions or ideas or
associations.

The impulse to use buildings as a means of supporting one's outlook on life has evidently been felt by architects and non-architects
alike. The difference between them is solely in the scope and scale of
their intentions. Architects are trained to convert every building into
a work (or quasi-work) of art. In the real world, it is sufficient to be
less encompassing, less extreme, less pretentious, and less exclusive.
Architects claim that the ability to design is their own unique spe-
cialty, but this seems plausible only because people generally have
been disengaged from the design of their own buildings, a process
that architects have abetted.

Looking back to a time when craftsmen provided a close link
between buildings and their communities, the common ability to
design is evident. The surround of a door, a staircase newel, a roof
gable – these have provided the occasion when the ordinary components of building were infused with visual interest. Similarly, the sort
of metaphors that architects stress have also been widely used. For
instance, immigrants to North America incorporated in their houses
images that recalled their ethnic origins: Scottish dormers in Nova
Scotia, steep gabled roofs over low stone walls in Quebec, pagoda
roofs on the West Coast. Even today, the same need for symbols can
be found in a mobile home, dressed up by a bow window, lace
curtains, miniature garden, and white picket fence.

Moreover, while over the centuries people have been virtually
divorced from the design of their houses by the intervention of
craftsmen, builders, and architects (so that, often, the only decision
left to them is the colour of their front doors), they still have a large
measure of control over their furnishings and their gardens. Garden-
ing is a widespread cultural activity that transcends gender, class,
and ethnic divisions.[5] It also involves the same sort and range of

aesthetic considerations that occupy architects. People might initially select plants for their desired characteristics and associations, but they are faced with more complex design choices as soon as they come to arrange them. These may be unstated. They may also be dealt with separately rather than as components of a comprehensive plan. But choices about use, arrangement, ambience, form, texture, colour, emphasis, specialization, ornamentation, or seasonal variation, involve factors ranging from broad philosophical questions, through personality differences, to matters of individual taste.

The same applies to household furnishings. While some items are dominated and limited by their professional design – refrigerators, for example – most are available in many different models. Their selection, combination, and arrangement stem from their purchaser's philosophy of life. For example, the choice of different styles of tables and chairs for kitchens and dining rooms, discloses a hierarchy of rituals where some are valued more highly than others. An increasing size of television screen suggests a diminishing separation between the personal and media worlds of illusion and reality. Larger beds and baths mark a change in sexual attitudes. Wall-to-wall carpeting and rugs provide competing images of class and affluence. Shaping these choices are broader paradigms of meaning. The status of the living room, for example, has varied so that in one set of circumstances its formal ceremonies have been allocated to a front parlour reserved for special occasions, while in another context its informal activities have been removed to a recreation or family room. Ultimately guiding all these considerations is the overriding notion of home itself, which has accrued its significance, summed up in the adage 'home is where the heart is,' from five hundred years of use.[6] In other words, furnishings are not bought for their utility alone, or even just for their visual interest, although that has always been considered a basic aspect of design. They are both a manifestation of a society's way of viewing things, and a symbolic representation of the particular people who choose them.[7] That is, they explore exactly the same spiritual territory as architecture does.

Furthermore, there is no reason to believe that architects feel more deeply about buildings than people generally do about their gardens and furnishings. The difference is that architects (and their interpreters) are more extreme in their claims and more verbose about them. People rely to a great extent on unspoken traditions, precedents, and norms. They do not want to be constantly stimulated by powerful emotions or visionary ideas. They carry on their everyday lives below the threshold of such intense experiences. Architects are taught that every building ought to be conceived as 'architecture,' with all the mystique that the term commands. But much less is needed to touch our senses, minds, memories, feelings, or even our souls.

The problem is how to realize this affinity between people and their surroundings. Gardens and house furnishings may readily be left to their owners to resolve. Buildings are too complex and require specialized skills to produce. While people can choose from an extensive variety of plants or furnishings to construct their own symbolic surroundings, they are narrowly limited in their choice of buildings. They may share the same sort of aims and methods as architects in their own personal world, but must rely on architects to provide them with an equivalent public world. In these circumstances, architects are both the primary cause of the current situation and the key to its potential solution.

Architects certainly ought to be capable of designing buildings that respond to the community's requirements. They are the only persons trained to organize buildings three-dimensionally. They have some technical competence. They are well-versed in myth-making. And when the styles they adopt (like Neoclassicism or Modern) have not precluded diversity, or actually sanctioned it (like Art Deco or Post-Modern), they have shown that they are capable of being imaginative. Unfortunately, their preoccupation with stylistic dogma prevents them from methodically developing their expertise. It not only undermines the practical side of their work; it also reduces their ability to deal with the symbolic aspects of design. Architects do not explore how forms are transformed into symbols, but are driven to invent 'objective' symbols with 'universal' significance. To consider symbol-making as a human activity, capable of being investigated dispassionately, would recognize it as a normal social study devoid of moralizing judgments, and undermine its élitist mystique. The result is that architectural writers deal almost entirely with justifying particular products, and not with the purpose, method or process of their production.

Moreover, the ability of architects to conceive different solutions is inhibited by the idea that the value of their work is embodied in a personal or collective style that stands for a specific aesthetic philosophy. This teaches them to reject any forms that might be thought to compromise its unity, and to shun forms from other aesthetic systems. For architects, compromise is a mark of mediocrity rather than a reconciliation of diverse opinions. Its denunciation provides architects with the excuse to impose their views on other people and to refuse to accommodate other interests. Consequently, while architects are taught to be creative, this is within the narrow art-world context of inventing their own style or contributing to an existing one, rather than in the broader sense of being able to generate a variety or multiplicity of images and ideas.

None the less, at the present time, architects are the only group that the public can turn to in its pursuit of a more supportive environment. If they have been slow to offer solutions, they are at least familiar with the problems. To solve them, both the community and its architects must change their attitudes. People generally will have to become more aware of the importance of their surroundings so that their present indifference is replaced by active concern and involvement. Instead of passively accepting their exclusion from the process of determining the quality of the surroundings in which they live, they must exert the right to participate in their creation. The prevailing concern for the natural environment must be extended to include our own human-made environment.

It will probably be necessary to take the same path. People will have to overcome their long-standing lack of knowledge concerning the design of buildings and learn more about it so that they are able to interact with architects as equals. Responsibility for such a major component of social life cannot be left to a small professional class but must be accepted by the community as a whole. The architectural world continues to insist that its designs represent society, but this idea is a relic from the past and must be turned around if it is to reflect the present situation. We should no longer try to define a community in terms of its architects' architecture, but consider their architecture in terms of the community.

The design we give to buildings, and how we value it, provide an index of our culture. Historically, architects have imposed their own stamp on a significant part of our building environment, and projected their own characteristics on to society as a whole. They have decided how our buildings should portray us, and how we appear to ourselves: whether we are conformist or individualistic, conservative or radical, sober or flamboyant, witty or humourless; whether we support ethnic differences or cultural assimilation; whether our ties are local, national, or international; whether we view technology as our servant or master; whether we want to live in harmony with the natural environment, or to dominate and control it. Their work has made implicit statements about who and what and where we are. In a way, they have packaged our institutions and offered images of how we feel about aging, commerce, law, or education. They have indicated to us what we think of the past and hope for the future.

In providing their expertise, architects have added another layer to the information that all artefacts reveal concerning the time and place of their production. The truth or falseness of their contribution can be measured in the distance between the two sets of information and the values each depict. Where architects have imposed their own professional tastes and interests, and where these have been alien to the majority of the population, they have added little to the quality of the society in which they work. On the contrary, they have undermined its own sense of time, place, and identity by erecting symbols that were irrelevant or unsympathetic or foreign to its development. But where their designs have reflected, supported, enhanced, or expanded the conditions, circumstances, beliefs, values, ideals, aspirations, fantasies, or dreams of the community they served, they have enriched its way of life and given shape, substance, direction, and fulfilment to it.

From this preferred perspective, the future of architectural practice begins to emerge. The first step for architects is to abandon their outdated myths so that they can open their minds to other viewpoints. This will allow them to review their relationship with the public at large and encourage their cooperation with it. In this new situation, architects would no longer treat buildings as artworks but as social artefacts. Design would no longer be dictated by prescribed styles, but emerge from the solution of practical problems. The buildings that result, instead of being isolated monuments, would add incrementally to the overall improvement of the social fabric for its inhabitants.

The art-world practice of imposing its own works on the outside world has been largely a failure. The method is too bound up in architecture as an end in itself for architects, instead of as a means with a social purpose. It has proved too random (especially considering the vast expenditure of resources involved), too arbitrary (often in the pursuit of novelty), too esoteric, and too limited in its appeal. In contrast, the ordinary buildings that we construct and use already contain the elements of social meaning. The architect's responsibility is to help us as a society to take what is there, develop it, expose its possibilities, and make it visible and comprehensible. In one sense, then, architects have tried too hard. Usually buildings require little individual attention. Yet architects have come to admire most the sort of buildings that they seldom do – the very few buildings that find their way into the art-world inventory. Conversely, they like least the buildings that they normally work on – the everyday buildings that make up our towns and provide the reason for their professional existence.

It is a telling commentary on the current situation that architects must now be convinced that it is no mean achievement to design buildings that function well, and that allow people to carry on their social life in a practical way. This is not an easy task. Many of these buildings are large and complex, and the organization of their spaces, forms, structures, and mechanical equipment is difficult. The skills required for this work are unique, and are no less demanding or important than those of any other profession. If they have not been widely recognized, that is mainly because architects themselves, along with the history, theory, criticism, and education of the profession, have discounted this aspect of their own success, because of its lack of aesthetic interest for the advocates of a small art-world set.

Yet, paradoxically, if architects would simply give up their exaggerated view of what is expected of them, they would also be better able to help the community to achieve that extra element of design where it is needed. That is, by showing people how they can gratify their senses, stir their emotions, exercise their minds, or stimulate their imaginations, architects would enable others to get from buildings the same sort of pleasure, and support for their own tastes and beliefs, that is currently reserved for a particular group. What such buildings might look like is impossible to predict. The architectural creativity of most people has not yet been tapped. Moreover, their interests are just as likely as those of architects to change over time. The results will only emerge as they occur. In helping to form them, architects will surely learn to be proud of the service they provide. If they did, they would benefit not only themselves but also everyone else.

6.1 Architects attempt too much and achieve too little. Even a simple lighthouse can fulfil our dreams. If only architects would drop their outdated beliefs, they could help us create a more desirable environment.

Notes

1 The Problem

1 E.S. De Beer, 'Gothic: Origin and Diffusion of the Term; The Idea of Style in Architecture,' *Journal of the Warburg and Courtauld Institutes*, XI (1948), 147.

2 See, for example, the story about the Pruitt-Igoe housing in St Louis, Missouri, in Charles A. Jencks, *The Language of Post-Modern Architecture* (New York, 1977), 9.

3 Vincent Scully, 'A Search for Principle between Two Wars,' *RIBA Journal*, LXXVI (June 1969), 240–7.

4 'Mailer vs Scully,' *Architectural Forum*, CXX (April 1964), 96–7.

5 Robert Venturi, *Complexity and Contradiction in Architecture* (New York, 1966), 13. See *Architectural Design*, XLVII, no. 4 (1977), contents page: 'Several leading architects and architectural critics are of the opinion that the modern movement is at an end and that it is now being superseded by new work which they have taken to calling "post-modern."'

6 Peter Blake, *The Master Builders* (New York, 1960); Peter Blake, *Form Follows Fiasco* (Boston, 1977).

7 'Stacking the Decade Verbally,' *Progressive Architecture*, LX (December 1979), 58.

8 Arthur T. Bolton, *The Architecture of Robert and James Adam* (London, 1922), 100; John Ruskin, *The Works of John Ruskin*, ed. E.T. Cook and A. Wedderburn (London, 1903–12), IX, 438; Ulrich Conrads, ed., *Programs and Manifestoes on 20th-Century Architecture* (Cambridge, Mass., 1977), 22; Aldo Van Eyck, 'Rats Posts and Pests,' *RIBA Journal*, LXXXVIII (April 1981), 47–50.

9 Richard Pommer and Christian F. Otto, *Weissenhof 1927 and the Modern Movement in Architecture* (Chicago, 1991), 158, quotes Sigfried Giedion's report of a meeting where 'the idea was broached by Mies, I believe, that "the movement must now be cleaned up," ' and a number of people were named who would carry out the 'secret purification.'

10 Henry-Russell Hitchcock and Philip Johnson, *The International Style: Architecture Since 1922* (New York, 1932), 153, 148, 201.

11 Gunther Stamm, *The Architecture of J.J.P. Oud 1906–1963* (Tallahassee, Fla., 1978), 6.

12 Giorgio Vasari, *The Lives of the Painters, Sculptors and Architects*, ed. William Gaunt, trans. A.B. Hinds (London, 1970), IV, 177.

13 The Observer Surveys, *Architects* (London, 1964), 17.

14 Judith R. Blau, *Architects and Firms* (Cambridge, Mass., 1984), 66–7.

15 *Sunday Times* (24 September 1989), A2.

16 'Record Houses 1990,' *Architectural Record*, CLXXVIII (mid-April 1990), 33–101; *House Beautiful*, CXXXII (June 1990), 55–81. Circulation figures are from *Ulrich's International Periodicals Directory, 1991–92*, 30th ed., I 288, II 2376.

17 National Historic Preservation Act of 1966, preamble. See also James A. Glass, *The Beginnings of a New National Historic Preservation Program, 1957 to 1969* (Washington, 1990).

18 Rachel Carson, *Silent Spring* (Boston, 1962).

19 See, for example, Andrew Dobson, *Green Political Thought* (London, 1990).

20 *New York Times* (16 June 1978), 1.

2 Myth and Architecture

1 Carl-Martin Edsman, 'Stones,' *The Encyclopedia of Religion* (New York, 1987), XIV, 49–53.

2 H.J. Rose, *Religion in Greece and Rome* (New York, 1959), 178–81.

3 Vitruvius, *On Architecture*, trans. Frank Granger (London, 1970), IV, i.

4 Ibid, III, i.

5 E.H. Gombrich, 'Style,' *International Encyclopedia of the Social Sciences* (New York, 1968), XV, 354.

6 Vitruvius, I, iii.

7 Wladyslaw Tatarkiewicz, *A History of Six Ideas*, trans. Christopher Kasparek (The Hague, 1980), 121–52.

8 John Addington Symonds, *The Renaissance in Italy, The Fine Arts* (London, 1877), 4.

9 Gene Brucker, *Renaissance Florence* (New York, 1969), 223, estimated that two-thirds to three-quarters of the *male* population were not literate.

10 Spiro Kostoff, ed., *The Architect: Chapters in the History of the Profession* (New York, 1977), 59–95.

11 Eusebius Pamphili, *The Ecclesiastical History*, trans. J.E.L. Oulton (London, 1926–32), X, iv.

12 Erwin Panofsky, ed., *Abbot Suger on the Abbey Church of St. Denis and Its Art Treasures* (Princeton, 1946), 105.

13 Isabelle Hyman, ed., *Brunelleschi in Perspective* (Englewood Cliffs, N.J., 1974), 34–5.

14 Joan Gadol, *Leon Battista Alberti* (Chicago, 1969).

15 Leon Battista Alberti, *On the Art of Building in Ten Books*, trans. Joseph Rykwert, Neil Leach, and Robert Tavernor (Cambridge, Mass., 1988), prologue.

16 Ibid, VI, ii.

17 Rudolf Wittkower, *Architectural Principles in the Age of Humanism* (London, 1988), 47–51.

18 Alberti, IX, xi.

19 James S. Ackerman, *Palladio* (Harmondsworth, 1966).

20 Alberti, IX, v; Andrea Palladio, *The Four Books of Architecture* (New York, 1965), IV, ii.

21 Wittkower, *Architectural Principles*, 138.

22 Rudolf Wittkower, 'Genius: Individualism in Art and Artists,' *Dictionary of the History of Ideas*, ed. Philip P. Wiener (New York, 1973–4), II, 308; Ernest Kris and Otto Kurz, *Legend, Myth, and Magic in the Image of the Artist* (New Haven, 1979).

23 Giorgio Vasari, *The Lives of the Painters, Sculptors and Architects*, ed. William Gaunt, trans. A.B. Hinds (London, 1970), IV, 108.

24 See Alberto Pérez-Gómez, *Architecture and the Crisis of Modern Science* (Cambridge, Mass., 1983) for some of its history.

25 Myra Nan Rosenfeld, 'The Royal Building Administration in France from Charles V to Louis XIV,' in Kostoff, *The Architect*, 161–79.

26 Anthony Blunt, *Art and Architecture in France, 1500 to 1700* (Harmondsworth, 1988) 222–34.

27 Arthur Drexler, ed., *The Architecture of the École des Beaux-Arts* (New York, 1977); Donald Drew Egbert, *The Beaux-Arts Tradition in French Architecture* (Princeton, 1980); Robin Middleton, ed., *The Beaux-Arts and Nineteenth-Century French Architecture* (Cambridge, Mass., 1982).

28 Perrault described it as 'the Desire they have, that the things of their

Profession should seem to have Mysteries, of which, they themselves
are the only Expositors.' Claude Perrault, *A Treatise of the Five Orders
in Architecture*, trans. John James (London, 1722), xvi.

29 Ibid, passim.

30 Baldesar Castiglione, *The Book of the Courtier*, trans. Charles S. Single-
ton (Garden City, N.Y., 1959), 77–82.

31 Daniel Cotton, 'Taste and the Civilized Imagination,' *Journal of Aesthetics and Art Criticism*, XXXIX (Summer 1981), 367–80.

32 David Hume, 'Of the Standard of Taste,' *Four Dissertations* (New
York, 1970), 201–40.

33 Samuel H. Monk, *The Sublime* (Ann Arbor, Mich., 1960); David
Watkin, *The English Vision* (London, 1982).

34 Edmund Burke, *A Philosophical Enquiry into the Origin of Our Ideas of
the Sublime and Beautiful*, ed. J.T. Boulton (London, 1958), part 2.

35 Leon Pompa, *Vico, a Study of the 'New Science,'* (Cambridge, 1975);
Erich Auerbach, 'Vico and Aesthetic Historicism,' *Journal of Aesthetics
and Art Criticism*, VIII (December 1949), 110–18.

36 Johann Bernhard Fischer von Erlach, *Entwurff einer historischen archi-
tectur* (Vienna, 1721).

37 John Harris, *Sir William Chambers* (London, 1970).

38 Dorothy Stroud, *George Dance, Architect 1741–1825* (London, 1971).

39 Elizabeth Gilmore Holt, ed., *A Documentary History of Art* (New York,
1958), II, 360–1.

40 Horace Walpole, *Anecdotes of Painting in England* (London, 1782), I, v.

41 For a discussion of early *Zeitgeist* theory, see Isaiah Berlin, *Vico and
Herder* (London, 1976), 68 passim.

42 'Noli me tangere,' *European Magazine*, LXII (November 1812), 381.

43 E.H. Gombrich, *The Story of Art* (London, 1950), chap. 23, and numerous other editions over the following decades.

44 A.W.N. Pugin, *Contrasts* (Leicester, 1969).

45 John Ruskin, *The Works of John Ruskin*, ed. E.T. Cook and A. Wedderburn (London, 1903–12), VIII, 24.

46 E.E. Viollet-le-Duc, *Lectures on Architecture*, trans. Benjamin Bucknall
(London, 1877–81), I, 242 passim.

47 Peter Collins, *Changing Ideals in Modern Architecture, 1750–1950*
(Montreal, 1965), 128–46.

48 M.F. Hearn, ed., *The Architectural Theory of Viollet-le-Duc: Readings and
Commentary* (Cambridge, Mass., 1990), 9–10.

49 For an early essay on the merits of originality, see Edward Young,
Conjectures on Original Composition (Leeds, 1966).

50 John Soane, *Lectures on Architecture*, ed. Arthur T. Bolton (London, 1929), 122.

51 In Roman terminology, a client was a dependant of a patron. About the 15th century, lawyers seem to have turned this usage upside down by calling their employers their clients, thereby altering the perception of the location of power between them. Other professions adopted the term that suggests that their employers are obligated to them, rather than the other way around. See *Oxford English Dictionary*, 2nd ed., s.v. 'client.'

52 Barrington Kaye, *The Development of the Architectural Profession in Britain* (London, 1960), 47; Roger Dixon and Stefan Muthesius, *Victorian Architecture* (New York, 1978), 10–11.

53 For example, many governments subsidize art-world activities with public funds.

54 H.J. Eysenck, 'Psychology of Art,' (in part), *Encyclopedia of World Art* (London, 1966), XI, 768.

55 For various views on psychology and art, see David O'Hare, ed., *Psychology and the Arts* (Brighton, Sussex, 1981).

56 George David Birkhoff, *Collected Mathematical Papers* (New York, 1950), III, 320–64, 382–535.

57 Ibid, 329.

58 Eysenck, 'Psychology of Art,' 774. Eysenck radically altered Birkhoff's formula to read $M = O \times C$ so that it would conform more closely to his experimental data. See also H.J. Eysenck, *Sense and Nonsense in Psychology* (Harmondsworth, 1970), chap. 8.

59 For an extreme example of the attempt to 'prove' that 'art' is a biological function, see D.E. Berlyne, *Aesthetics and Psychobiology* (New York, 1971). Berlyne's 'evidence' ranged from Praxiteles to Jackson Pollock.

60 Horatio Greenough, *Form and Function*, ed. Harold A. Small (Berkeley, 1947), 65.

61 Louis H. Sullivan, *Kindergarten Chats* (New York, 1947), 208.

62 Ibid; Henry Wotton, *The Elements of Architecture* (London, 1624), 1.

63 See Larry L. Ligo, *The Concept of Function in Twentieth-Century Architectural Criticism* (Ann Arbor, Mich., 1984), 5, for a list of types of function.

64 Robert Owen, *The Life of Robert Owen* (New York, 1967), I, 62.

65 Oscar Newman, *CIAM '59 in Otterlo* (Stuttgart, 1961), 30. In this statement, the inference is that design can not only support a desired mode of behaviour, but actually modify it. The idea was not so

appealing to right-minded critics when manifested in consumer research and the introduction of environmental devices to encourage consumers to buy merchandise. Oscar Newman went on to write *Defensible Space: Crime Prevention through Urban Design* (New York, 1972), a much quoted study linking design and behaviour.

66 Richard Neutra, *Survival through Design* (New York, 1954), 202.

67 The staff of the Building Research Station in Britain included sociologists and psychologists by the 1950s. See F.M. Lea, *Science and Building: A History of the Building Research Station* (London, 1971), 98.

68 For example, A.S. Baum, 'Environmental Psychology,' *Encyclopedia of Psychology*, ed. Raymond J. Corsini (New York, 1984), I, 441–3.

69 See, for example, the articles related to buildings in Jack L. Nasar, ed., *Environmental Aesthetics: Theory, Research, and Applications* (Cambridge, 1988).

70 For an attempt to explain the ideological reasons why architects adopted this stance, see Alan Lipman, 'The Architectural Belief System and Social Behaviour,' *British Journal of Sociology*, XX (June 1969), 190–204.

71 Le Corbusier, *Towards a New Architecture*, trans. Frederick Etchells (London, 1927).

72 Le Corbusier, *The Modulor*, trans. Peter de Francia and Anna Bostock (London, 1954), 56.

73 Ulrich Conrads, ed., *Programs and Manifestoes on 20th-Century Architecture* (Cambridge, Mass., 1977), 109. Other leaders of the Modern style had their own inflated claims. Mies van der Rohe proclaimed that 'architecture is the will of the age conceived in spatial terms'; Gropius, that it is the 'crystalline expression of man's noblest thoughts, his ardour, his humanity, his faith, his religion.' See ibid, 74, 46.

74 *Architects' Journal*, CXXXV (21 March 1962), 617, 619–20.

75 See, for example, Alexandra Tyng, *Beginnings, Louis I. Kahn's Philosophy of Architecture* (New York, 1984).

76 Heinz Ronner, Sharad Jhaveri, Alessandro Vasella, *Louis I. Kahn: Complete Works 1935–74*, (Boulder, Col., 1977), 449.

77 Renato Poggioli, *The Theory of the Avant-Garde* (Cambridge, Mass., 1968).

78 For example, Camilla Gray, *The Great Experiment: Russian Art 1863–1922* (New York, 1962), 215.

79 Le Corbusier, *My Work*, trans. James Palmes (London, 1960), 147.

80 Tod A. Marder, ed., *The Critical Edge* (Cambridge, Mass., 1985),

163–74; Paul Goldberger, 'Architects Meet to Note Failures of Modernism,' *New York Times* (11 December 1980), III, 19.

81 Gavin Macrae-Gibson, *The Secret Life of Buildings* (Cambridge, Mass., 1985), 96.

82 Paul Goldberger, 'The Museum That Theory Built,' *New York Times* (5 November 1989), II, 1; *New York Times* (10 May 1989), III, 21.

3 Architecture and Culture

1 See A.L. Kroeber and Clyde Kluckhohn, *Culture: A Critical Review of Concepts and Definitions* (Cambridge, Mass., 1952). The authors state that the modern meaning of the word evolved during the second half of the 19th century and was summarized in 1871 in the defining statement of E.B. Tylor that culture 'includes knowledge, belief, art, law, morals, custom, and any other capabilities and habits acquired by man as a member of society.'

2 Denys Hay, *Europe: The Emergence of an Idea* (Edinburgh, 1957).

3 Henri Baudet, *Paradise on Earth*, trans. Elizabeth Wentholt (New Haven, 1965).

4 Johann Gottfried von Herder, *Reflections on the Philosophy of the History of Mankind*, ed. Frank E. Manuel (Chicago, 1968).

5 Hans Kohn, *Nationalism, Its Meaning and History* (Princeton, 1965).

6 Vitruvius, *On Architecture*, trans. Frank Granger (London, 1970), VI, i.

7 J.J.Winckelmann, *History of Ancient Art*, trans. G. Henry Lodge (New York, 1968), II, iv, first published in 1764. The importance of climate had been stated previously in Montesquieu's *The Spirit of Laws* (1748), where, for example, Montesquieu recommended that suicide in Britain should not be considered a crime because the weather there drove people to it.

8 Kevin Harrington, *Changing Ideas on Architecture in the 'Encyclopédie,' 1750–1776* (Ann Arbor, Mich., 1985).

9 J.W. von Goethe, 'Of German Architecture,' *A Documentary History of Art*, ed. Elizabeth Gilmore Holt (New York, 1958), II, 361–9.

10 E.E. Viollet-le-Duc, *Lectures on Architecture*, trans. Benjamin Bucknall (London, 1877–81), I, 244.

11 Friedrich von Schlegel, *The Aesthetic and Miscellaneous Works of Frederick von Schlegel*, trans. E.J. Millington (London, 1849), 169.

12 M.H. Port, ed., *The Houses of Parliament* (New Haven, 1976), 30.

13 John Soane, *Lectures on Architecture*, ed. Arthur T. Bolton (London, 1929), 149.

14 Talbot Hamlin, *Benjamin Henry Latrobe* (New York, 1955), 274.

15 A sense of national pride had earlier led the architect Delorme (1567) and Louis XIV's minister Colbert (1672) to propose new French Orders as befitting a nation that had become as great as those of antiquity. See Anthony Blunt, *Philibert de L'orme* (London, 1958), 118–22; Joseph Rykwert, *On Adam's House in Paradise* (Cambridge, Mass., 1981), 77.

16 A.W.N. Pugin, *Contrasts* (Leicester, 1969), 2.

17 Peter Davey, *Arts and Crafts Architecture* (London, 1980).

18 W.R. Lethaby, *Philip Webb and His Work* (London, 1979).

19 Hermann Muthesius, *The English House*, ed. Denis Sharp, trans. Janet Seligman (London, 1979), 11.

20 Edward Robert Robson, *School Architecture* (London, 1874), 71.

21 Mark Girouard, *Sweetness and Light* (Oxford, 1977).

22 Andrew Saint, *Richard Norman Shaw* (New Haven, 1976).

23 H.H. Statham, 'Architecture, Part 1. Modern,' *Encyclopedia Britannica* (1875–1903), XXV, 588.

24 *American Architect and Building News*, XVII (13 June 1885), 282.

25 James F. O'Gorman, 'The Marshall Field Wholesale Store,' Society of Architectural Historians, *Journal*, XXXVII (October 1978), 175–94. Also James F. O'Gorman, *H.H. Richardson, Architectural Forms for an American Society* (Chicago, 1987).

26 Carl W. Condit, *The Chicago School of Architecture* (Chicago, 1964), 52–4; Donald Hoffmann, *The Architecture of John Wellborn Root* (Baltimore, 1973), 67–8.

27 Louis H. Sullivan, *Kindergarten Chats* (New York, 1947), 30.

28 Louis H. Sullivan, *The Autobiography of an Idea* (New York, 1926).

29 Sherman Paul, *Louis Sullivan* (Englewood Cliffs, N.J., 1962), 1–3; Narcisco G. Menocal, *Architecture as Nature: The Transcendentalist Idea of Louis Sullivan* (Madison, Wis., 1981).

30 Sullivan, *Kindergarten Chats*, 202–13.

31 Frank Lloyd Wright, 'In the Cause of Architecture,' *Architectural Record*, XXXV (May 1914), 407.

32 David F. Burg, *Chicago's White City of 1893* (Lexington, Ky., 1976), 112.

33 James Philip Noffsinger, *The Influence of the École des Beaux-Arts on the Architects of the United States* (Washington, 1955).

34 Theo B. White, ed., *Paul Philippe Cret, Artist and Teacher* (Philadelphia, 1973).

35 Leland M. Roth, *McKim, Mead and White, Architects* (New York, 1983).

36 J.B. Bury, *The Idea of Progress* (New York, 1920); Robert A. Nisbet, *History of the Idea of Progress* (New York, 1980).

37 A.L. Millin, *Dictionnaire des beaux-arts* (Paris, 1806), I, 53, cited in Peter Collins, *Changing Ideals in Modern Architecture, 1750–1950* (Montreal, 1965), 65.

38 Leon Battista Alberti, *On the Art of Building in Ten Books*, trans. Joseph Rykwert, Neil Leach, and Robert Tavernor (Cambridge, Mass., 1988), VI, iii.

39 Meyer Schapiro, 'Style,' in *Anthropology Today*, ed. A.L. Kroeber (Chicago, 1953), 288.

40 For a related critique of the *Zeitgeist* theory from another standpoint, see David Watkin, *Morality and Architecture* (Oxford, 1977).

41 G.B. Vico, *The New Science of Giambattista Vico*, trans. T.G. Bergin and M.H. Fisch (Ithaca, N.Y., 1968), 63.

42 Anthony Jackson, *The Politics of Architecture* (London, 1970).

43 Anthony Blunt, *Art and Architecture in France, 1500 to 1700* (Harmondsworth, 1988).

44 John Summerson, *Architecture in Britain 1530–1830* (Harmondsworth, 1983).

45 Nikolaus Pevsner, *Pioneers of the Modern Movement* (London, 1936).

46 Sigfried Giedion, *Space, Time and Architecture* (Cambridge, Mass., 1941).

47 Henry-Russell Hitchcock and Philip Johnson, *The International Style: Architecture Since 1922* (New York, 1932).

48 Sibyl Moholy-Nagy, *Moholy-Nagy, Experiment in Totality* (New York, 1950), 97–8, 246–7.

49 *Charter of the United Nations* (1945), Article 1.

50 As of September 1993, the number of United Nations members was 184 and still rising. See *The World Almanac and Book of Facts, 1994* (Mahwah, N.J., 1993), 834.

51 Patrick Conner, *Oriental Architecture in the West* (London, 1979).

52 Philip Davies, *Splendours of the Raj* (London, 1985).

53 European Association for Architectural Education, *Architectural Education in Europe and the Third World: Parallels and Contrasts* (Newcastle upon Tyne, 1984).

54 Tanizaki Jun'ichiro, *In Praise of Shadows*, trans. T.J. Harper and E.G. Seidensticker (New Haven, 1977).

55 Norma Evenson, *Chandigarh* (Berkeley, 1966), 6.

56 Oscar Newman, *CIAM '59 in Otterlo* (Stuttgart, 1961), 147–8.

57 Ibid, 80–6.

58 Alison Smithson, ed., 'Team 10 Primer,' *Architectural Design*, XXXII (December 1962).

59 Newman, *CIAM '59*, 208.

60 The most effective critique was by Brent C. Brolin, *The Failure of Modern Architecture* (New York, 1976). A decade later, when Chandigarh's population was about 450,000, Ravi Kalia, *Chandigarh: In Search of an Identity* (Carbondale, Ill., 1987), 152, wrote: 'There are two cultures in Chandigarh – the culture of buildings and monuments and the culture of the people. The two cultures are different in content, and the monuments and buildings do not represent the spirit of the people.'

61 Lawrence Alloway, 'The Development of British Pop,' in Lucy R. Lippard, *Pop Art* (New York, 1966), 32.

62 Robert Venturi, Denise Scott Brown, Steven Izenour, *Learning from Las Vegas* (Cambridge, Mass., 1977), 85.

63 Robert Venturi, *Complexity and Contradiction in Architecture* (New York, 1966); 102.

64 Charles W. Moore, 'Plug It in, Rameses, and See if It Lights up, Because We Aren't Going to Keep It Unless It Works,' *Perspecta 11*, (1967), 33–43; Eugene J. Johnson, ed. *Charles Moore, Buildings and Projects 1949–1986* (New York, 1986).

4 Culture and Class

1 Leon Battista Alberti, *On the Art of Building in Ten Books*, trans. Joseph Rykwert, Neil Leach, and Robert Tavernor (Cambridge, Mass., 1988), VI, iii.

2 Andrea Palladio, *The Four Books of Architecture* (New York, 1965), III, xx.

3 See chap. 3, n. 7.

4 William Chambers, *A Treatise on the Decorative Part of Civil Architecture*, 3rd. ed. (London, 1791), 19–21.

5 Théophile Gautier, *Mademoiselle de Maupin*, trans. Joanne Richardson (Harmondsworth, 1981), preface. César Graña and Marigay Graña, eds., *On Bohemia: The Code of the Self-Exiled* (New Brunswick, N.J., 1990).

6 George H. Ford, *Dickens and His Readers* (New York, 1974), 7.

7 A.W.N. Pugin, *Contrasts* (Leicester, 1969), illustration, 'Catholic Town in 1440' and 'The Same Town in 1840.'

8 Great Britain, House of Commons, Select Committee on Arts and Their Connexion with Manufactures, *Report* (London, 1836).

9 Adrian Forty, *Objects of Desire* (London, 1986), 29–41 passim. Also the

Wedgwood catalogue of 1787 for the improvement of public taste argument.

10 Select Committee on Arts, *Report*, 24–5.

11 Stuart Macdonald, *The History and Philosophy of Art Education* (New York, 1970); Quentin Bell, *The Schools of Design* (London, 1963).

12 Great Britain, House of Commons, Select Committee on the School of Design, *Report* (London, 1849), iv.

13 Ibid, xv.

14 *The Crystal Palace Exhibition* (New York, 1970), xiii–xv; Tobin Andrews Sparling, *The Great Exhibition: A Question of Taste* (New Haven, 1982).

15 Elizabeth Bonython, *King Cole* (London, 1982).

16 Yvonne ffrench, *The Great Exhibition: 1851* (London, 1950).

17 Great Exhibition of the Works of Industry of All Nations, 1851, *Official Descriptive and Illustrated Catalogue* (London, 1851), I, 18–19.

18 Exhibition of the Works of Industry of All Nations, 1851, *Reports by the Juries* (London, 1852), I, xvi.

19 Ibid, see Richard Redgrave, 'Supplementary Report on Design.'

20 Susan P. Casteras and Ronald Parkinson, eds., *Richard Redgrave 1804–1888* (New Haven, 1988), 36.

21 Great Britain, Department of Practical Art, *First Report* (London, 1853), 2.

22 Ibid, 33.

23 'A House Full of Horrors,' *Household Words*, VI (4 December 1852), 265–70.

24 Great Britain, Committee of Council on Education, Science and Art Department, *Twentieth Report* (London, 1873), xiv.

25 Great Britain, Committee of Council on Education, Science and Art Department, *Forty-Sixth Report* (London, 1899), xxv.

26 Great Britain, Council for Art and Industry, *Education for the Consumer* (London, 1935).

27 Macdonald, *Art Education*, 349–52.

28 See Raymond Williams, *Culture and Society 1780–1950* (Harmondsworth, 1961), for a seminal discussion of the topic.

29 William Morris, *Selected Writings and Designs*, ed. Asa Briggs (Harmondsworth, 1962), 30.

30 Ian Bradley, *William Morris and His World* (London, 1978); J.W. Mackail, *The Life of William Morris* (London, 1899).

31 John Ruskin, *The Works of John Ruskin*, ed. E.T. Cook and A. Wedderburn (London, 1903–12), X, 196.

32 Peter Floud, 'The Inconsistencies of William Morris,' *The Listener*, LII (14 October 1954), 615–17.

33 Philip Henderson, *William Morris* (New York, 1967), 274–5.
34 Linda Parry, *William Morris Textiles* (London, 1983), 60, 70.
35 Henderson, *William Morris*, 76–7.
36 Ruskin, *Works*, XXIX, 154.
37 See William Morris, *News from Nowhere* (London, 1890).
38 George Bernard Shaw, *William Morris as I Knew Him* (New York, 1936), 16.
39 *Journal of Design and Manufactures*, II (September 1849), 72.
40 Dudley Harbron, *The Conscious Stone* (New York, 1971), 95.
41 Moncure D. Conway, 'Bedford Park,' *Harper's New Monthly Magazine*, CCCLXX (March 1881), 482.
42 Mark Girouard, *Sweetness and Light* (Oxford, 1977); Elizabeth Aslin, *The Aesthetic Movement* (New York, 1981).
43 Peter Davey, *Arts and Crafts Architecture* (London, 1980).
44 Joan Campbell, *The German Werkbund* (Princeton, 1978).
45 Reyner Banham, *Theory and Design in the First Machine Age* (London, 1960), 68–78; Open University, History of Architecture and Design 1890–1939, *Documents*, ed., Charlotte Benton (Milton Keynes, 1975), 6–11.
46 Alan Windsor, *Peter Behrens* (London, 1981); Tilmann Buddenseig, ed., *Industriekultur: Peter Behrens and the AEG, 1907–1914*, trans. Iain Boyd Whyte (Cambridge, Mass., 1984).
47 Hans M. Wingler, *The Bauhaus*, trans. Wolfgang Jabs and Basil Gilbert (Cambridge, Mass., 1969); Frank Whitford, *Bauhaus* (London, 1984).
48 John Nelson Tarn, *Five Per Cent Philanthropy* (Cambridge, 1973), 43.
49 Mervyn Miller, *Raymond Unwin: Garden Cities and Town Planning* (Leicester, 1992).
50 Hermann Muthesius, *The English House*, ed. Dennis Sharp, trans. Janet Seligman (London, 1979), 58–60.
51 Nicholas Bullock and James Read, *The Movement for Housing Reform in Germany and France 1840–1914* (Cambridge, 1985).
52 Ronald Wiedenhoeft, *Berlin's Housing Revolution: German Reform in the 1920s* (Ann Arbor, Mich., 1985).
53 Paul F. Wendt, *Housing Policy – The Search for Solutions* (Berkeley, 1963), 117.
54 See, for example, Ruskin's letters to a 'working man' in Ruskin, *Works*, XVII, 321, 430.
55 Iain Boyd Whyte, *Bruno Taut and the Architecture of Activism* (Cambridge, 1982), 55–60.

56 Barbara Miller Lane, *Architecture and Politics in Germany, 1918–1945* (Cambridge, Mass, 1968), 102.

57 Wiedenhoeft, *Berlin's Housing Revolution*, 30.

58 London County Council, *London Housing* (London, 1937).

59 Catherine Bauer, *Modern Housing* (Boston, 1934), 148.

60 Frank Lloyd Wright, *Modern Architecture* (Princeton, 1931), 65–7, 101–2.

61 For example, Walter Curt Behrendt, *Modern Building: Its Nature, Problems and Forms* (New York, 1937), 196–208.

62 Museum of Modern Art, *Modern Architecture* (New York, 1932), 192.

63 Hermann Muthesius, 'Post-War Architecture in Germany,' *RIBA Journal*, XXXIII (16 October 1926), 593.

64 Dora Wiebenson, *Tony Garnier: The Cité Industrielle* (New York, 1969).

65 Le Corbusier, *The City of Tomorrow*, trans. Frederick Etchells (London, 1929), 102.

66 Ulrich Conrads, ed., *Programs and Manifestoes on 20th-Century Architecture* (Cambridge, Mass., 1977), 144.

67 Royal Institute of British Architects, *International Architecture 1924–1934* (n.d.), 10.

68 Russell Lynes, *The Taste-Makers* (London, 1954), 310–33. See Virginia Woolf, *The Death of the Moth* (London, 1942), 113–19, who proposed an alliance between 'highbrows' who lived through their ideas, and 'lowbrows' who lived through their work, against 'middlebrows' who had no interest in either art or life.

69 Helena Barrett and John Phillips, *Suburban Style* (London, 1987). See also the perceptive essay on British suburbs by the advocate of Modern architecture, J.M. Richards, *The Castles on the Ground* (London, 1946).

70 C. Wright Mills, *White Collar* (New York, 1951).

71 'The FORTUNE Survey,' *Fortune*, XXI (February 1940), 14 passim.

72 William H. Whyte, *The Organization Man* (New York, 1956).

73 Lewis Mumford, *The City in History* (New York, 1961), 486, 494.

74 Clement Greenberg, 'Avant-Garde and Kitsch,' *Partisan Review*, VI (Fall 1939), 40.

75 Dwight Macdonald, *Masscult and Midcult* (New York, 1961).

76 Angus Maddison, *Phases of Capitalist Development* (Oxford, 1982), 92.

77 Ronald Inglehart, *The Silent Revolution* (Princeton, 1977), table 7–8.

78 U.S. Bureau of the Census, *Historical Statistics, Colonial Times to 1870* (Washington, 1975), Series H602–17, H751–65.

79 The process may be followed from its AIA First Honor Award in 1952, through Reyner Banham, *Guide to Modern Architecture* (London,

1962), 98, to Charles Jencks, *Modern Movements in Architecture* (Garden City, N.Y., 1973), 41, 200.

80 As pointed out by Deyan Sudjic, *Cult Heroes* (London, 1989), 92, the building was featured on the front page of the *New York Times* (31 March 1978) and the *Times* of London (13 May 1978), and the cover of *Time* magazine (8 January 1979).

81 See, for example, John Fiske, *Understanding Popular Culture* (Boston, 1989), 20–1.

5   Class and Architects

1 Patricia Mainardi, 'Quilts: The Great American Art,' in *Feminism and Art History: Questioning the Litany*, ed. Norma Broude and Mary D. Garrard (New York, 1982).

2 Marian W. Smith, ed., *The Artist in Tribal Society* (London, 1961).

3 Plato, *Phaedrus*, trans. R. Hackworth (Cambridge, 1952), 57–61.

4 Giorgio Vasari, *The Lives of the Painters, Sculptors and Architects*, ed. William Gaunt, trans. A.B. Hinds (London, 1970), I, 66.

5 Benvenuto Cellini, *The Autobiography of Benvenuto Cellini*, trans. George Bull (Harmondsworth, 1956).

6 See Rudolf Wittkower and Margot Wittkower, *Born under Saturn* (London, 1963), for a background history, and Vytautas Kavolis, 'Artistic Cultures,' *Encyclopedia Britannica* (1986), XIV, 120–3, for a classification, of art-making types.

7 Donald W. MacKinnon, 'The Nature and Nurture of Creative Talent,' *American Psychologist*, XVII (July 1962), 484–95.

8 Alfred Barry, *The Life and Works of Sir Charles Barry* (London, 1867), 87; Alfred Hoyt Granger, *Charles Follen McKim* (Boston, 1913), 108; Andrew Saint, *Richard Norman Shaw* (New Haven, 1976), 312.

9 Arthur Clason Weatherhead, *The History of Collegiate Education in Architecture in the United States* (New York, 1941); Caroline Shillaber, *Massachusetts Institute of Technology School of Architecture and Planning 1861–1961* (Cambridge, Mass., 1963).

10 Johannes Itten, *Design and Form*, trans. John Maass (New York, 1964).

11 Marcel Franciscono, *Walter Gropius and the Creation of the Bauhaus in Weimar* (Urbana, Ill., 1971), 195.

12 Laszlo Moholy-Nagy, *The New Vision*, trans. Daphne M. Hoffmann (New York, 1932).

13 Ibid, 158.

14 As an example, see *New York Times* (10 May 1990), III, 1, 12.

15 A requirement enacted in Britain in 1931, and extended throughout the U.S.A. by 1951. See Andrew Saint, *The Image of the Architect* (New Haven, 1983), 91, 150.

16 For example, the program at the University of Bombay, in the 1980s, covered the standard architectural history of the West, including the 'Pioneers of Contemporary Architecture' – Wright, Le Corbusier, Gropius, Mies van der Rohe.

17 Donald Albrecht, *Designing Dreams* (New York, 1986).

18 Aldo Rossi, *The Architecture of the City*, trans. Diane Ghirardo and Joan Ockman (Cambridge, Mass., 1982).

19 For example, Howard Robertson, *The Principles of Architectural Composition* (London, 1924). 'Unity' was illustrated by the Doge's Palace, Venice, and King's Cross Station, London; 'Character,' by the Gothicized *Chicago Tribune* skyscraper and the glass-walled Hallidie Building, San Francisco.

20 Herbert J. Gans, 'Toward a Human Architecture: A Sociologist's View of the Profession,' in *Professionals and Urban Form*, ed. Judith R. Blau, Mark E. La Gory, John S. Pipkin (Albany, N.Y., 1983), 303.

21 Statistics Canada, *Employment Income by Occupation* (Ottawa, 1993), 8–9, 14–15. The average incomes of fully employed *male* architects, civil engineers, and visual artists were $53,083, $50,389 and $22,396. For females, they were $36,083, $38,137, and $14,533. One other factor is that more architects were self-employed than civil engineers.

22 See, for example, Donald J. Treiman, *Occupational Prestige in Comparative Perspective* (New York, 1977); Robert W. Hodge, Paul M. Siegel, and Peter H. Rossi, 'Occupational Prestige in the United States, 1925–63,' *American Journal of Sociology*, LXX (November 1964), 290.

23 *The Fountainhead* (1949), director King Vidor, from the novel by Ayn Rand.

24 Heinz Eulau and John D. Sprague, *Lawyers in Politics* (Westport, Conn., 1984), 11. Robert L. Nelson and John P. Heinz, 'Lawyers and the Structure of Influence in Washington,' *Law and Society Review*, XXII (1988), 238, calculated that, in 1983, 60 per cent of the members of the Senate and 44 per cent of the members of the House of Representatives, were lawyers.

25 Laurin A. Wollan, 'Lawyers in Government – 'The Most Serviceable Instruments of Authority,' *Public Administration Review*, XXXVIII (March/April 1978), 106.

26 Geoffrey Mills, *On the Board* (London, 1985), 266.

27 Jeremy Bacon, *Corporate Directorship Practices: Membership and Committees of the Board* (New York, 1973), 29.

28 *Contemporary Architects*, ed. Ann Lee Morgan and Colin Naylor (Chicago, 1987), 990–2.

29 Frank Schaffer, *The New Town Story* (London, 1970), 56; L. Hugh
   Wilson, 'A New Approach to a New Town,' *Architects' Journal*, CXXV
   (17 January 1957), 86.

30 This is reminiscent of the score card drawn up by the 18th-century art
   theorist, Roger de Piles, to measure painters and their 'Degrees of
   Perfection.' Michelangelo received 37 points out of a possible 80. See
   Elizabeth Gilmore Holt, ed., *A Documentary History of Art* (New York,
   1958), II, 186.

31 National Endowment for the Arts, *Arts Participation in America:
   1982–1992* (Washington, 1993), iii.

32 *Canadian Arts Consumer Profile, 1990–1991, Findings* (1992), 258, 266,
   estimated that about two-thirds of the audience for ballet and contemporary dance were female.

33 For example, Canada Council, *A Survey of Arts Audience Studies: A
   Canadian Perspective 1967–1984* (Ottawa, 1984), 43. See also its anno-
   tated bibliography and selected statistics from other countries.

34 In Canada, in 1990, there were 11,915 architects in a population of 26
   million. Statistics Canada, *Employment Income by Occupation*, 8–9.

35 Robert Gutman, *Architectural Practice: A Critical View* (Princeton, 1988),
   92–4. Even more than art, architectural criticism in newspapers has been
   dominated by a few individuals. For example, a whole generation of
   readers of the *New York Times*, for thirty years from the early 1960s to
   the early 1990s, received its information on the subject of architecture
   mainly through the eyes of Ada Louise Huxtable and Paul Goldberger.

36 Great Britain, Department of Education and Science, *Art for Ages 5 to
   14* (1991).

37 Library of Congress, *Subject Headings*, 13th ed., (1990), III, 3342.

38 Herbert J. Gans, *Popular Culture and High Culture* (New York, 1974).
   See also Herbert J. Gans, 'Popular Culture in America: Social Problem
   in a Mass Society or Social Asset in a Pluralist Society,' in *Social Problems: A Modern Approach*, ed. Howard S. Becker (New York, 1966).
   Robert Woods Kennedy, *The House and the Art of Its Design* (New
   York, 1953), 18–21, had observed earlier that there were five types of
   clientele influencing the design of American houses, with support for
   the Modern style that he used being limited mainly to a section of the
   upper middle class.

39 L. Moholy-Nagy, *Vision in Motion* (Chicago, 1947), 98–9. See also Paul
   Oliver, ed., *Shelter and Society* (London, 1969), 20–1.
40 Sibyl Moholy-Nagy, *Native Genius in Anonymous Architecture in North
   America* (New York, 1957).
41 For example, Charles, Prince of Wales, *A Vision of Britain* (London,
   1989).
42 Christopher Alexander, *The Timeless Way of Building* (New York, 1979);
   Christopher Alexander, Sara Ishikawa, Murray Silverstein with Max
   Jacobson, Ingrid Fiksdahl-King, Shlomo Angel, *A Pattern Language*
   (New York, 1977); Christopher Alexander, Hajo Neis, Artemis
   Anninov, Ingrid King, *A New Theory of Urban Design* (New York,
   1987).
43 J.M. and Brian Chapman, *The Life and Times of Baron Haussmann* (London, 1957); Anthony Sutcliffe, *The Autumn of Central Paris* (London,
   1970), 346, 181.
44 U.S. Housing Act of 1949, sec. 105.
45 U.S. Housing and Home Finance Agency, *How Localities Can Develop a
   Workable Program for Urban Renewal* (Washington, 1955), 10–11.
46 J. Clarence Davies, *Neighborhood Groups and Urban Renewal* (New York,
   1966), 72–109.
47 Jane Jacobs, *The Death and Life of Great American Cities* (New York,
   1961).
48 16 & 17 Elizabeth II, c.72, sec. 3; Great Britain, Ministry of Housing
   and Local Government, *People and Planning* (London, 1969).
49 C. Richard Hatch, ed., *The Scope of Social Architecture* (New York,
   1984), 186–200.
50 Peter Collymore, *The Architecture of Ralph Erskine* (London, 1982),
   12–13.
51 *Scope of Social Architecture*, 166–85.
52 *Charles Moore, Buildings and Projects 1949–1986*, ed. Eugene J. Johnson
   (New York, 1986), 47–53.
53 Sherry R. Arnstein, 'A Ladder of Citizen Participation,' *Journal of the
   American Institute of Planners*, XXXV (July 1969), 217.
54 Nick Wates and Charles Knevitt, *Community Architecture* (Harmondsworth, 1987), 116.

6 Architects and Design

1 See, for example, Susan Saegert, 'Masculine Cities and Feminine Suburbs: Polarized Ideas, Contradictory Realities,' in *Women and the Amer-*

ican City, ed. C.R. Stimpson, E. Dixler, M.J. Nelson, K.B. Yatrakis (Chicago, 1981).

2 Warren Hunting Smith, *Architecture in English Fiction* (New Haven, 1934).

3 For example, Fiske Kimball and George Harold Edgell, *A History of Architecture* (New York, 1918), 503–4.

4 John A. Kouwenhoven, *The Columbia Historical Portrait of New York* (Garden City, N.Y., 1953), 394–5. Note Montgomery Schuyler's remark in his 1897 article 'The Sky-line of New York' that 'it is in the aggregation that the immense impressiveness lies.' In the 100 years since, the buildings have changed considerably but the effect has remained the same.

5 T. Stephens and C.L. Craig, *The Well-Being of Canadians: Highlights of the 1988 Campbell's Survey* (Ottawa, 1990), 57. See also Witold Rybczynski, *Waiting for the Weekend* (New York, 1991), 199–209.

6 The *Oxford English Dictionary*, 2nd ed., gives this definition of *home*: 'The place of one's dwelling or nurturing, with the conditions, circumstances, and feelings which naturally and properly attach to it, and are associated with it,' and cites its first use in the 15th century.

7 See Mihaly Csikszentmihalyi and Eugene Rochberg-Halton, *The Meaning of Things* (Cambridge, 1981).

Picture Credits

Index

Numbers in italic refer to illustration pages.